...redefined the meaning of womanhood. Today, ..."feminist" label, but have nonetheless absorbed ...drug coursing through the vein of an uncon- ...ght has thoroughly permeated our culture. In ... ...ing, and relevant book, Carolyn McCulley encourages us to wake up and become radical—to live as biblically savvy women in the modern world. It's an excellent read and a stirring challenge!

MARY A. KASSIAN
Distinguished Professor of Women's Studies,
The Southern Baptist Theological Seminary
Author, *The Feminist Mistake*

Few voices are speaking the truth contained in these pages—but so many need to hear it. Amidst our culture's radical confusion about womanhood, Carolyn teaches the radical truth of God's wise and gracious design for women. And as Carolyn's friends for many years, we can attest that her personal example fully supports what she teaches here. Her book—and her life!—reflect careful insight, humble honesty, and gospel-centered wisdom. Women young or old, married or single, will be instructed and inspired by this book.

C. J. AND CAROLYN MAHANEY
Sovereign Grace Ministries
Authors of *The Cross-Centered Life* and *Feminine Appeal*

As a young woman, Carolyn McCulley eagerly embraced many of the tenets of our "feminist world." A personal encounter with Christ radically changed her life and led her to pursue what it means to live as a redeemed woman. This book is the fruit of her journey. Her keen observations and thoughtful analysis explain the seismic shift brought about in our culture by the feminist revolution. Her biblical insight makes this a valuable resource for women who want to fulfill their created mission and live out the radical implications of the Gospel in a fallen world.

NANCY LEIGH DEMOSS
Author, *Lies Women Believe*
Host, *Revive Our Hearts* radio

Here is a helpful, biblical, straightforward, engaging and compelling book that sets out a biblical vision for womanhood. I am so thankful that my friend Carolyn McCulley has written it. She represents the scores of godly, young, Christian women who are thoughtfully rejecting the world's notion of the "New Woman" and who are, instead, joyfully embracing the Scripture's teaching on the "True Woman." Carolyn was once deeply influenced by feminist thinking, but came to see the bankruptcy of that worldview. She wants you to understand why much of what women learn about what it means to be a woman in today's culture (whether it is taught in college, read or heard via the media, or assumed in society) leads to a dead end. More importantly, she wants you to know why the Bible's view of womanhood inspires joy and peace.

LIGON DUNCAN
Senior Minister, First Presbyterian Church, Jackson, Mississippi, USA
President, Alliance of Confessing Evangelicals
Chairman, Council on Biblical Manhood and Womanhood
Past Moderator, Presbyterian Church in America
Adjunct Professor, Reformed Theological Seminary

Radical Womanhood is a subversive message of a better way for women. With courage, clarity, history and stories that stick, Carolyn delicately dismantles the shrines of feminism with the glories of biblical femininity. Ladies, grab a coffee, a corner and listen to Carolyn talk about how God's Word transforms women.

DAVE HARVEY
Sovereign Grace Ministries
Author, *When Sinners Say "I Do"*

How wonderful when biblical clarity and conviction expose and replace worldly confusion and deception. Radical Womanhood does just this on the profound impact of feminism within our culture and particularly upon the church. Carolyn McCulley combines solid research along with engaging personal testimony (her own and that of others) to give a clear picture of feminism's influence over the past two centuries. Carolyn traces the first, second, and third waves of feminist ideology, and discusses how these ideas have influenced all of us more than we might have ever known. The foundation of this discussion is God's Word, and Carolyn regularly demonstrates how God's eternal truth is the answer to feminism's questions and confusion. We highly recommend this book to discern God's abiding truth as it relates to one of the most powerful deceptions of our age.

BRUCE AND JODI WARE
The Southern Baptist Theological Seminary

In this carefully researched and clearly written book, Carolyn McCulley exposes the historical roots and contemporary bitter fruits of the Feminist movement. She shows that in contrast the truly radical way to affirm femininity is to adopt the Biblical perspective on womanhood. This is a book that needs to be read by all women - and by men too!

IAIN DUGUID
Professor of Old Testament, Grove City College

RADICAL *Womanhood*

FEMININE FAITH *in a* FEMINIST WORLD

Carolyn McCulley

MOODY PUBLISHERS

CHICAGO

Cover Design: The DesignWorksGroup
Cover Image: Shutterstock #3449451
Interior Design: Ragont Design
Editor: Dana Wilkerson

Library of Congress Cataloging-in-Publication Data

McCulley, Carolyn, 1963-
  Radical womanhood : feminine faith in a feminist world / Carolyn McCulley.
     p. cm.
  Includes bibliographical references (p.   ).
  ISBN 978-0-8024-5084-5
  1. Women--Religious aspects--Christianity. 2. Feminism--Religious
aspects--Christianity. 3. Christian women--Religious life. I. Title.
  BT704.M54 2008
  270.082--dc22
                                    2008026545

                    ISBN: 978-0-8024-5084-5

We hope you enjoy this book from Moody Publishers. Our goal is to provide high-
quality, thought-provoking books and products that connect truth to your real needs
and challenges. For more information on other books and products written and produced from a biblical perspective, go to www.moodypublishers.com or write to:

                    Moody Publishers
                820 N. LaSalle Boulevard
                    Chicago, IL 60610

                1 3 5 7 9 10 8 6 4 2

            Printed in the United States of America

Dedicated with love to my family:
James and Rosalind McCulley,
Fred and Alice Barber,
and Andrew and Beth Oman.

With special thanks for your patience during my years of feminism
and your loving support during the writing of this book.
I am deeply grateful for you all!

CONTENTS

FOREWORD

"Why hasn't anyone ever told us this before?" That was the question the audience of college-aged Christian women asked Carolyn McCulley, and that is the reason she wrote this outstanding book. Carolyn explains her transition from a 30-year old secular feminist, thoroughly influenced by modern culture's expectations about women, to a young Christian seeking to understand the Bible in its teachings about womanhood, sexuality, marriage, family, and children

Carolyn recognizes that today a younger generation of Christian women is eager to hear the great teachings of the Bible on the equal value of men and women, and on the beauty of our differences as planned and created by God.

Carolyn mixes together some great ingredients in this book: (1) a deep and wise understanding of the Bible's teachings on men and women; (2) fascinating historical narratives about the lives of feminist leaders from the past two centuries; (3) wonderfully encouraging stories about contemporary people who have made a transition from radical feminism, or prostitution, or abusive backgrounds, or marital unfaithfulness, to serving Jesus Christ with deep commitment and joy; and (4) a great writing style that will hold a reader's interest from the first page to the last. This is an excellent book!

I have taught and written extensively on the topic of biblical manhood and womanhood for the last 23 years, and Carolyn's writing is certainly consistent with those writings. But Carolyn also asked if I could mention how biblical manhood and womanhood have worked out in my own marriage.

Margaret and I were married June 6, 1969, which means that we have now been married for 39 years. There have been ups and downs, as with any marriage, but looking back now at those 39 years, we have more joyful, wonderful memories than we can count. And today we love to be together, enjoying time with friends, or in our church, or traveling together, or just having a half-hour "date" by going grocery shopping together. I walk down a different aisle to get an item, then I look for Margaret, and my heart is happy to see her again! What great blessings God gives to those who follow his Word!

Earlier this month we were back in Libertyville, Illinois, and we had some free time, so we drove by all four of the houses we had owned during the twenty years we lived there from 1981 to 2001. In every neighborhood and on every street we recalled happy memories of raising our three sons in Libertyville, taking them to soccer or baseball practice, playing touch football with them, watching them get their first jobs so they could pay for car insurance, getting to know their friends in elementary school or high school, or just going together to walk the dog – the ordinary things of life! Why was there such blessing from God during those 20 years? I think because God helped Margaret and me to pattern our marriage after the teachings of the Bible, the same teachings that Carolyn so clearly expresses in this book.

Tomorrow we are going to meet our three sons, and two daughters-in-law, and one beautiful young granddaughter, on a family vacation. We are watching their lives with joy because they too are seeking to follow the Bible's patterns for husbands and wives and children. "Blessed is everyone who fears the Lord, who walks in his ways!" (Psalm 128:1).

In our own marriage, I seek to make wise decisions in my role as the "head" (see Eph. 5:24), and I seek to love Margaret "as Christ loves the church" (Eph. 5:25). And Margaret seeks to "submit" to my leadership as the Bible says (see Eph. 5:22). But a day does not go by when she does not also give me wise counsel and advice and encouragement to be faithful to the Lord. And I listen! I have written over a hundred pages of scholarly articles on the meaning of the Greek word for "head" in the verse, "The husband is the head of the wife even as Christ is the head of the church" (Eph. 5:23), but one day I realized that a well-functioning head has two ears! Those are for the purpose of listening to your wife! Leadership while listening with love works out in small family decisions and sometimes in large ones, such as when we decided to move to Arizona in 2001.

A few years before that, when we were still living in Illinois, Margaret began to experience chronic pain as a result of an earlier auto accident. We didn't think there was any medical solution, but then some friends invited us to use their second home in Mesa, Arizona (a suburb of Phoenix). We stayed a few days in the hot, dry climate, and Margaret felt better! A few months later we returned for a second visit, and she felt better again. It turned out that her pain was aggravated by cold and humidity – and the Chicago area where we lived was cold in the winter and humid in the summer! But Arizona was dry and warm.

I told Margaret, "I'd be happy to move here, but I don't think there would be any way for me to get a job here. I'm only trained to do one thing—be a professor at a theological seminary. And there aren't any seminaries in the Phoenix area."

The next day, just out of curiosity, Margaret was looking in the Yellow Pages under "Educational Institutions," and she said, "Wayne, there is something here called Phoenix Seminary." Then I remembered that I had heard something about a new, small seminary in the Phoenix area. We checked it out, and one thing led to another, and I eventually phoned and asked if there was a possibility they would have a job for me. They said yes!

But it meant a career shift. At the time (2001) I had been a professor at Trinity Evangelical Divinity School in Deerfield, Illinois, for twenty years. I had the rank of Professor (the highest rank), I had tenure (which pretty much guarantees a job for life), and I was department chairman I the department of Biblical and Systematic Theology (a department with 8 faculty members). Trinity had over 1500 students, a strong Ph.D. program in which I could teach, and it had the reputation of being one of the very finest academic institutions in the evangelical world.

By contrast, Phoenix Seminary was young and small, with about 200 students and eight faculty members in the whole seminary. Should I agree to make the change? When the day came that I had set apart to consider this before the Lord, I opened my Bible to the next passage I would come to in my regular reading through the Bible, and my eyes fell on Eph. 5:28, "In the same way husbands should love their wives as their own bodies." I thought, "If my body were experiencing the pain that Margaret is experiencing, would I decide to move to Phoenix?" I thought, yes, I would move for the sake of my own body. Then shouldn't I also move for the sake of Margaret's body?" So I was willing to move, for Margaret's sake.

But then I found out that she wanted to stay in Illinois, for the sake of the ministry God had given me at Trinity. We were both concerned for the other person's welfare – I think that's how marriage is supposed to function. At that point Phoenix Seminary phoned and said they wanted to make me a "Research Professor" with reduced teaching hours and more time to write, and with that, Margaret agreed that it might be a blessing for both of us to move.

What should the final decision be? We prayed and talked and went for walks and talked some more. Finally Margaret said, "I have made up my mind what to do about this decision." I said, "What?" She said, "I have decided that you should make the decision!" I smiled, but I also felt the burden of the responsibility. It seems to me that that is how marriage is supposed to function – prayer and love and conversation, and each caring for the other, but then, finally, the husband as head of the household has responsibility to make the decision. My decision was that we should move, for the sake of Margaret's health.

In the seven years we have lived in Arizona, God has again brought abundant blessing. The seminary has grown, purchased a beautiful building, acquired a good library, and gained full accreditation. I have seen significant blessing on my teaching and writing ministry. God has given us a wonderful church and special friends and many opportunities for ministry. Margaret has found abundant opportunity to minister to younger women in our church, and to seminary wives, and also to many others. God has given us great joy in our marriage. And Margaret feels a lot better! I'm not saying there are no difficulties—Margaret had a knee replaced last year and it still has not fully healed, so there are some challenges. But we have the great joy of walking in God's ways each day, and we look forward to perhaps another 20 or 30 years of marriage! "Blessed are the people whose God is the Lord!"

WAYNE GRUDEM
July 31, 2008

PREFACE

*T*his is the book I wish someone had given me on my thirtieth birthday.

I had just returned from a holiday in South Africa where, quite unexpectedly, I had found myself listening to a preacher explain why Jesus Christ lived and died. The next thing I knew, I was going to church every Sunday. I knew something profound had happened to me on that trip, but becoming a Christian was the last thing this party girl expected to happen.

So there I was, lost in the land of church ladies—women wearing floral prints and long skirts, holding a baby on each hip, and appearing happy to be homemakers. I'm sure I was gawking like a tourist at a zoo. I'm sure they were tempted to gawk back, too, for I was an obvious newbie. I was the brash, single professional woman far more familiar with the latest issue of *Cosmopolitan* magazine and the alternative music scene than I was with the Bible or any hymns or praise choruses.

How well I remember those first months of culture shock in that church. As a new Christian, I had an entirely new worldview to process and evaluate: people were actually reading the Bible! And *believing* it! They talked about relationships and roles so differently from anything I had ever heard before. Part of me wanted to run away, and part of me was greatly intrigued.

I've never forgotten what that experience was like. That's why I wrote this book. I wrote it for my thirty-year-old self, the woman who needed to understand why much of what she had been taught in college and read in the media led to a dead end, and why the Bible inspired joy and peace. I hope these pages will also save numerous readers a few years of asking, "Why?" and learning lessons the hard way, as I did.

More importantly, I wrote this book for the girls I addressed many years later at a regional conference for college students. Trying to gauge their understanding of the various items I was referencing in my message, I asked for a show of hands as I mentioned people or events.

"How many of you have heard of the suffrage movement?" A few hands went up. "How about Betty Friedan? Gloria Steinem?" Again, only a sprinkling of raised hands. "Simone de Beauvoir or Jean-Paul Sartre?" Maybe one hand—way in the back.

"What about the Proverbs 31 woman?" To my surprise, again, only a few hands shot up at this Christian conference.

"Okay, then. Well, how many of you are children of divorce?" More than half of the women in the room raised their hands.

At that point, I realized I was talking to a generation living with the fallout of seismic cultural change, *but they didn't know what had happened!* (They also didn't know what was in the Bible—an alarming thought for a Christian event, though not entirely unexpected for so many new believers.) Seeing their need, I set aside my speaking notes and began to address them with passion. I explained to them what previous generations had done to change the definition of being a woman. I talked to them about all that they had inherited—both benefits and the detriments. I talked to them about what the Bible had to say on these matters. And then I challenged them to be different, to live as biblically savvy women in the modern world.

When it was over, many of them came forward to say this information was all brand-new to them. "Why hasn't anyone ever told us this before?" they asked.

I hope some of them find this book one day so they can know

more than what I could explain in only one hour. I want them to understand what is *truly* radical about being a woman in the image of God.

In the meantime, you're the one holding this book. I'm grateful that you are and hope that you find much eye-opening information and sound counsel within these pages. In each of the following chapters, you'll read a bit of history, a commentary from Scripture, and the story of a woman who has found God to be true to His Word. I know all of these women, but for the sake of their privacy I have changed their names and some of their identifying details. They live in different cities and attend different churches, but along with me they share a common testimony about their faithful God.

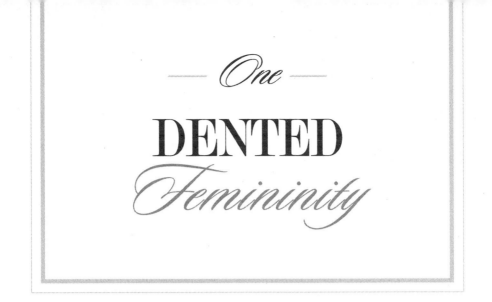

One
DENTED
Femininity

*T*he first time you hear a boy say it, it can sting.

"You throw like a *girl!*"

"He screamed just like a girl!"

"Ewwww . . . that's gross. It's pink. That's girl stuff."

The content of these insults usually lacks any serious substance, but the implication is clear: girls are different. As in, worse. Inferior. If a boy is lacking skill, strength, or speed, he is no better than a . . . *girl*.

From deep within the feminine heart, a primordial protest erupts: *That's not fair!*

I don't know when this concept dawned on me, but it must have been during grade school. I have memories of competing in field day races and wanting to make sure the all-girl teams did well against the all-boy teams. At one point, the boys were given a few freedoms at recess that the girls didn't get—perhaps to play some contact sport. So we girls bunched up around the teacher on recess duty and sarcastically played childish kindergarten games to make our point.

By high school, the gender divide became more threatening—and, bizarrely, more alluring. Every girl wanted the attention traditionally paid to cheerleaders or prom queens, but there was always the risk of locker-room gossip. Girls in high school were no longer accused of having cooties or just being "gross." By this stage, masculine insults contained a threatening, disrespectful edge, often laced with sexual slander. Yet, some guys were just plain cute. We wanted their compliments and time. We just didn't know if we could trust them. And sometimes we couldn't.

This roughly summarizes my understanding of "sexual politics" until college—nothing traumatic or really even mildly dramatic. My family was intact and stable. My father was loving and active in my life, as was my mother. I was involved in lots of school activities. My parents came to every concert, marching band performance, school play, and parent-teacher conference. I floated on the fringes of the popular crowd—not part of the inner sanctum of cheerleaders and football players but close enough to be invited to the occasional party.

None of that really explains why I ended up in that first women's studies class at college. It's likely I thought it would be an easier elective than political science or economics. But the reason I took the next women's studies class was much more purposeful: through feminism, I had been handed a worldview that addressed the covert sexism I had suspected all these years. Things were beginning to click. The problem was . . . *men*! "Patriarchy" and its oppression of women were the true culprits. (Um, make that *womyn*.) As a journalism major, I needed some topic to specialize in, a cause to champion. I found mine in feminism. I made it my life's mission then to splash the cause of feminism across magazines and airwaves wherever I worked.

There were little skirmishes along the way. Sometime in college, as I recall, my growing feminism ruined Thanksgiving. During dinner, my uncle, a no-nonsense Naval Academy graduate, made some comment—now long forgotten and probably more benign than I recognized—to which I took great offense. I began a tirade about rape, patriarchy, the oppression of "womyn," and the suffocating roles of wives and mothers. (None of which, with the exception of patriarchy, had I personally experienced.) Any refutation of my sweeping condemnations was met with increased volume and passion on my part. I had lived a mere two decades, but in my opinion I possessed the wisdom of the ages.

Then there was the time I stunned my father with the announcement that if I were ever to marry, I wasn't going to change my last name. At the time, I thought it was a repressive and unnecessary tradition, and I didn't see any reason to change my identity just because I would obtain a husband. I honestly thought my father would champion my idea because he was the father of three daughters and if we all changed our names, the family name would die with him. But he didn't seem pleased, which genuinely surprised me. In hindsight I honestly don't know if it was the information or my attitude that provoked his reaction.

I learned a lot of theory in women's studies classes, but surprisingly, I didn't learn a lot of actual history. We learned about the women's liberation movement of the 1960s and 1970s, but not anything earlier. I don't recall studying anything written prior to Betty Friedan's influential book from the 1960s, *The Feminine Mystique* . . . , which is to say, nothing earlier than my own lifetime. It would be years before I learned about the suffrage movement that preceded modern feminism, the differing impacts of the Reformation and Enlightenment on gender roles, and, finally, what the Bible says about men and women.

Feminism taught me that men were the problem, but in the end feminist politics left me yawning. While I had no problem agreeing that men in general were the problem, individual and specific men seemed far more agreeable and even attractive to me. After awhile, the strident victimhood of feminism lost its appeal. Though one of my fellow graduates went to work for feminist political action groups—the National Organization for Women (NOW) and then the Feminist Majority—I took my journalism diploma and my women's studies certificate and pursued a career in media.

It wasn't long before my definition and practice of feminism became as generic as that of the next woman clutching *Cosmopolitan* magazine. Social constructs and gender theories were dim memories. I was left with androgynous "dress for success" fashion, a hyperperception of sexual harassment and discrimination on the job, and a caricature of masculine sexuality as a model of freedom for both sexes. Aggression at work and on dinner dates was the legacy of my education.

When I was twenty-nine, I surveyed my life and perceived the emptiness of it. A relentless self-focus hadn't produced much happiness.

The Fractured Feminine Psyche

During this time, a friend of mine lent me a book, telling me how helpful it was for "reclaiming a whole feminine psyche." The book's premise was that women could be restored by studying the weaknesses and strengths of the goddesses from Greek mythology and by seeking to reconcile these archetypes into one complete woman.

I took the test in the book and found out that I tested very high as Athena, the warrior goddess who sprung fully formed from the head of Zeus. This is the section of the summary that I noted in my journal at the time:

> It's easy to spot Athena in the modern world. She's out there in every sense of the word. Editing magazines, running women's studies departments in colleges, hosting talk shows, making fact-finding tours to Nicaragua, producing films, challenging the local legislature.
>
> The Athena woman is very visible because she is an extravert, she's practical, and she's intelligent. Men are often a little intimidated by her at first because she doesn't respond to the usual sexual gambits and she will push them to the wall in any intellectual argument. When they have won her respect, she can be the most loyal of companions, a lifelong friend, and a generous fund of inspiration. . . .
>
> Despite her strength, brilliance, and independence, there is a paradox contained in the traditional image of a maid clad in armor. It seems to us that the more energy the Athena woman puts into developing her successful, worldly, armored self, the more she hides her maidenly vulnerability. So, with her androgyny, Athena conceals a conflict, an unresolved tension between her tough outer self and her hidden, unexpressed self that can be a source of great insecurity with regard to her finding an integral feminine identity. We call it Athena's wound. . . .
>
> She will spar with [her mate], compete with him, and often despise him because he is not as tough as she is.[1]

That was a fairly accurate portrait of my life then. I really didn't know what to do with my feminine identity, but I certainly knew how to spar with men. Now, in quoting that book, I'm not endorsing it in any way. But I do look back and marvel at how creative God is when He begins to work in our hearts. Because I was nowhere near a Bible at the time, God used that book and its faulty psychological premise to jump-start my thinking. That quote was the last thing I wrote in my journal before boarding a flight to South Africa. I left for that vacation thinking that I needed to do something to address my fractured feminine psyche. I saw the problem—or at least part of it—but I wasn't sure how to resolve it.

It was during my travels in South Africa that God revealed to me more about this dilemma and offered His priceless solution. I was going to visit my sister and brother-in-law, who were living there on a temporary basis to study at a Bible college. My plan was to enjoy an exotic holiday and nothing more. But on Easter Sunday, in a church pushing for racial reconciliation in a nation scarred by apartheid, I heard the greatest message of redemption and forgiveness that would ever reach human ears.

There, sitting among people who had once despised each other for the color of their skin, I learned that hope for change was found in the life and death of Jesus Christ. After explaining the historical evidence for the veracity of Jesus' life, the pastor told us the significance of His death. He started with the problem of sin—our rebellion against God's laws and holy standards. In a place like South Africa, wreaked by prejudice and bloodshed, sin is clearly evident. But even if we've never discriminated against anyone nor murdered anyone, we are not innocent. From the moment we screamed, "No!!" as a toddler to the times we have cheated, lied, and stolen as adults, to the innumerable hours we spend consumed about our self-image and self-assessment at the expense of others, we have accumulated a weight of guilt and sin that crushes us before a holy God.

The pastor explained to us that the Bible says that death is the consequence of sin. We each face death because of our individual sins, but we also live in a broken world because of our collective sinfulness. But God offers us a shocking solution. To break the cycle of sin and death, He sent His Son, Jesus Christ, to be our substitute—to live the perfect life that we cannot live in order to pay the punishment for our sins that we cannot pay. *Jesus died on the cross so that we could live.* His resurrection three days later was proof that His sacrifice was sufficient to break the curse of sin and death. God does not ignore sin or tolerate injustice. He poured all the righteous anger for our sins on His Son so that we could receive forgiveness. Sin does not go unpunished, but in the cross of Christ mercy triumphs over judgment. This is the gospel—or the good news—of Jesus Christ's life, death, and resurrection.

That Easter Sunday, I finally heard and understood the gravity of this message. I saw the anger, the harsh judgment of others, and the selfishness in my life for what it was: sin against God and against others. And I broke down in tears as the good news of Jesus' saving sacrifice was revealed and offered to me.

For the first time, I had real hope for change. But change was a process. I still straddled the fence in some areas, cynical about the evangelical subculture, televangelism scandals, faked miracles, and denominational division. Throughout the trip, I asked my sister and brother-in-law many tough questions. They responded graciously with the words of Scripture but did not try to sell me on their views. I marveled at their restraint and pondered their words as the dusty red roads of South Africa passed under our wheels.

On the third Sunday in South Africa, we visited a church in Cape Town to hear my brother-in-law's former pastor. An American by the name of C. J. Mahaney preached a message about the honesty and range of human emotions recorded in the Psalms. C. J. alleviated my concerns about turning into a fake smiley-face button for Jesus. The Bible did not shrink back from the reality of our fluctuating feelings. It also did not leave us wallowing in them. Our emotions were designed by God to propel us toward truth and faith—a progression modeled for us in nearly every psalm.

Submission Impossible

When I returned home, I knew God had done something in my life. Real faith was budding in my life, but I didn't know what this meant for me. I was different—but I still needed personal mentoring and instruction. I knew I needed to quit some obvious sin patterns, go to church, and read my Bible, but I wasn't convinced that a whole lot else needed to change. Little did I know that the Holy Spirit was in the process of turning me upside down and shaking loose all my prior beliefs and ideas like so much pocket change.

Point by point, the Holy Spirit used the Bible and the church to renew my mind. I conceded nearly every aspect until I reached one passage in Ephesians: "Wives, submit to your husbands as to the Lord. For the husband is the head of the wife as Christ is the head of the church, his body, of which he is the Savior. Now as the church submits to Christ, so also wives should submit to their husbands in everything" (5:22–24 NIV).

Submission?! Surely that was one ancient concept that no one practiced anymore! There was no way on God's green earth that I would ever concede that women are inferior and must live as second-class to men. That passage was just wrong, wrong, *wrong*. All my feminist offenses roused themselves in objection.

But I kept going to church.

That's when I began to hear my pastor and other people talking about another foreign concept: servant-leadership. The awkward phrasing of this concept demanded an explanation. Once again, I was pointed to Ephesians, chapter 5. This time, I read the rest of the offending passage. Though the first part was for wives, the verses that followed for husbands were far more challenging and provided a definition of leadership that was not for self-glory but for the benefit of another.

> *Husbands, love your wives, just as Christ loved the church and gave himself up for her to make her holy, cleansing her by the washing with water through the word, and to present her to himself as a radiant church, without stain or wrinkle or any other blemish, but holy and blameless. In this same way, husbands ought to love their wives as their own bodies. He who loves his wife loves himself. After all, no one ever hated his own body, but he feeds and cares for it, just as Christ does the church—for we are members of his body. "For this reason a man will leave his father and mother and be united to his wife, and the two will become one flesh." (5:25–31 NIV)*

This was not autocratic, self-glorifying leadership. This was leadership to serve God's purposes for the benefit of others.

Submission. Servant-leadership. Until that point in my life, these were foreign concepts to me. But before that Easter Sunday in South Africa, so was the third concept: sin. Though I was familiar with the word, it was one I applied to *other* people. Until I heard the gospel, I didn't see sin very clearly in myself. If I saw weaknesses, shortcomings, or failures in myself, I was good at blaming other people for them or minimizing them in me. I was blind to the sins of envy, anger, self-righteousness, judgment, greed, and pride that coursed through my daily actions.

The word I *did* know how to apply to myself was "self." I was all about myself and maximizing my own comfort, opportunity, and pleasure.

God's Wisdom for Women

Slowly it began to dawn on me that the Bible was not presenting just a new set of rules for successful relationships or a peaceful life. It was presenting an entirely new *game*—with radically different goals for victory. Winning was living a life that glorified God. Winning was growing in humility. Winning was trusting God and serving others. Winning was cultivating the fruit of the Spirit: love, joy, peace, patience, kindness, goodness, faithfulness, gentleness, and self-control (Galatians 5:22–23). Winning was growing in Christlikeness.

All my previous feminist philosophies resulted in merely kicking at the darkness, expecting it would bleed daylight. But Scripture says that it is by God's light that we see light (Psalm 36:9). *The light of God's Word showed me truth*. What I thought was right and true didn't hold up to Scripture. Human observation and psychology could only point out the problem—proud women spar with men they deem to be weaker and not worthy of respect—but offered no credible solution to the tension between the sexes.

I didn't need to reconcile my pantheon of inner goddesses. I needed to repent of my sin.

As do men.

The kicker is that feminism is partially right. Men do sin. They can diminish women's accomplishments and limit women's freedoms for self-centered reasons. Some men sexually assault women. Some men abuse their wives and children. Many men degrade women through pornography. Feminism didn't rise up because of fabricated offenses. As one theologian said, it is understandable, humanly speaking, why this movement did emerge:

> When you realize that men have subjugated women for thousands of years, you can only wonder how it took so long for the feminist movement to form. It is unfortunately rare to find a marriage in which the husband recognizes that he bears the responsibility of headship and exercises it in humility and love rather than force and authoritarianism. While I too am against so much of what the feminist movement advocates, I understand why it has emerged. I believe that if Christian men had been the servant leaders in the home, rather than conceited chauvinists, the feminist movement would have died a quick and easy death. If men had sought ways to see the gifts and talents of their wives developed and utilized rather than taking a beautiful person and making her into little more than a personal slave, if men had not twisted this doctrine of headship, we would not have the current problems between men and women in our society. . . . I am tired of hearing that feminists are responsible for the breakdown of the family. We need to put the responsibility where it belongs—on the heads of homes.[2]

I agree, but as this book is for women and not men, I'll leave it to the guys to challenge each other. My concern is what we've absorbed from our culture about being women. Feminism (like most other "isms") points a finger at other people for the problems of life. But I learned that Scripture tells us that other people are not the real problem. Our sinful nature (James 4:1–3), spiritual forces of evil (Ephesians 6:12), and the lure of this present world (1 John 2:15–17) are our real problems. But for me—and many women in this present age—the definition, practices, and contours of femininity are where the battles rage. What does it mean to be a woman and not a man? What is the significance of our ability to bear children? How should we handle our sexuality? Should we structure our careers just like men do? What's the purpose of being a wife?

There are competing answers out there. More than forty years after "women's lib" began, pundits claim that we now live in a post-feminist age. Feminism is a given. We breathe it, think it, watch it, read it. Whenever a concept so thoroughly permeates a culture, it's hard to step back and notice it at work. Feminism has profoundly altered our culture's concept of what it means to be a woman. We need to understand how this movement came about and what its goals have been because these are now our culture's assumptions. We also need to acknowledge that there has been some good that has come out of it. There were some serious inequities that were changed by the feminist movement. I'm grateful for the short-term gains, but the long-term consequences are profound and need to be examined in light of feminism's worldview.

My personal history is no doubt different from yours. You may not identify yourself as a current or former feminist. You may not identify yourself as a Christian—or, conversely, you may have grown up in the church. But chances are that there are aspects of your femininity that have been negatively impacted by feminism, no matter how you identify yourself now. That's why I believe it is important to examine the history of feminism, how it has affected our culture and our churches, and how its claims stand up to the teaching of Scripture.

This is the book I wished I had as a new believer. Over the years, I've tried to retain the impressions and memories I had as a new believer regarding the church, God, the Bible, masculinity, and femininity, just in case I had the opportunity to write it. When I first encountered these concepts as a new Christian, I wanted someone to explain to me how feminism came about, how it influenced my thinking, and why femininity as defined by the Bible wasn't a throwback to some horrible era. No one around me in the church *looked* unhappy, constricted, or oppressed by the gender roles described in the Bible. In fact, they were surprisingly joyful. The men treated me respectfully. The women smiled and laughed. The children were friendly and generally obedient. No one seemed lobotomized and I never did find any secret cult meetings. So after awhile, I accepted that this was genuine behavior and not a conspiracy to brainwash me into backwoods thinking. That left me free to examine the claims of Scripture without suspicion.

Fifteen years later, I am deeply grateful for the opportunity to write the book I looked for as a new believer—a book that examines the history of the feminist movement and its major philosophies and gives an explanation of what the Bible teaches about women, our worth, and our roles. If you are a new believer, or even if you are not a Christian, I pray that when you are finished with this book you will put it down with a better understanding of why God made men and women in His image—two sexes, equal in worth and dignity—and why He assigns different roles to us in order to accomplish His purposes in His kingdom.

If you are a longtime Christian, I pray you will be refreshed in your commitment to these godly principles. Biblical womanhood is not a one-size-fits-all mold. It's not about certain dress styles, Jane Austen movies, tea parties, quiet voices, and exploding floral patterns . . . or whatever stereotype you are picturing right now. To live according to biblical principles today requires women to be bold enough to stand against philosophies and strongholds that seek to undermine God's Word and His authority.

You've read part of my story already. In future chapters, you'll meet other women from different churches, backgrounds, and ethnicities—in other words, this book is not just drawn from my experience. I know all of these women, some for more than a decade. These are real women who have trusted God in joy and in sorrow. They join me in celebrating feminine faith in a feminist world.

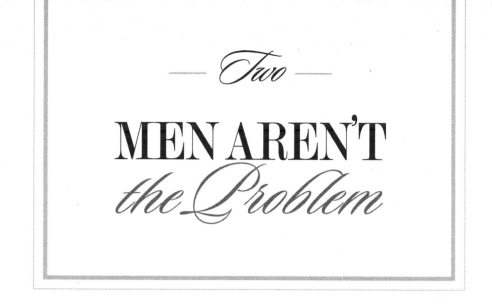

Two

MEN AREN'T
the Problem

*I*n the preface, I mentioned speaking to a group of college-aged women at a conference. Essentially, I was giving an overview of this book. That's an impossible amount of information to cram into an hour! It was hard not to just sling dates and names at them in rapid-fire succession. I feel the same way even with this book—there's so much information to sift through and present. That's why I've chosen to develop this material topically. Each chapter of this book addresses different aspects of women's lives and how competing definitions of womanhood have shaped those areas.

In this chapter, I introduce some of the basic history of feminism through the lives of three influential women: Elizabeth Cady Stanton, Simone de Beauvoir, and Betty Friedan. If you are a young woman, a lot of this may be new information to you. Hang in there through the history lesson, because it's important to know how we got to where we are today. Some of you, like myself, lived through part of this history but not with the clarity that hindsight brings. I trust this overview will help you to see how what happened in the nineteenth century became the impetus for the turbulence of the twentieth century. What follows is an introduction of how feminism came to identify men as the chief problem of women—and then how those issues are addressed by the Bible.

THERE'S A DIFFERENCE BETWEEN restoring God-
given rights to women and setting women above both men and God.
The history of the feminist movement shows that one led to another—and much earlier than the 1960s. In order to understand the
gender confusion of the 21st century, you have to rewind past the
girl-power movement of the 1990s, the women's liberation movement of the 1970s, the suburban domesticity of the 1950s, the Rosie-
the-Riveter era of World War II, the sexual brazenness of the Jazz Age,
and even the nineteenth-century push for women's right to vote, right
back to the founding of our nation.

   During this heady time, as the political concepts of democracy and
emancipation were taking shape in a new republic, women had high
hopes that they would receive equal legal status to men as citizens of
the United States of America. As Abigail Adams looked on all the fierce
political rhetoric in 1776, she implored her husband not to forget the
ladies. In a letter to John Adams on March 31, she made this plea:

> I long to hear that you have declared an independency. And, by the
> way, in the new code of laws which I suppose it will be necessary for
> you to make, I desire you would remember the ladies and be more
> generous and favorable to them than your ancestors. Do not put such
> unlimited power into the hands of the husbands. Remember, all men
> would be tyrants if they could. If particular care and attention is not
> paid to the ladies, we are determined to foment a rebellion, and will
> not hold ourselves bound by any laws in which we have no voice or
> representation.
>
> That your sex are naturally tyrannical is a truth so thoroughly es-
> tablished as to admit of no dispute; but such of you as wish to be
> happy willingly give up the harsh title of master for the more tender
> and endearing one of friend. Why, then, not put it out of the power of
> the vicious and the lawless to use us with cruelty and indignity with
> impunity? Men of sense in all ages abhor those customs which treat us
> only as the vassals of your sex; regard us then as being placed by Provi-
> dence under your protection, and in imitation of the Supreme Being
> make use of that power only for our happiness.

Unfortunately, her pleas fell on deaf ears. For as close and loving a marriage as they had, John Adams simply wrote back this teasing reply on April 14: "As to your extraordinary code of laws, I cannot but laugh."[1]

As radical as her ideas might have sounded to her husband, Abigail was not suggesting that women should throw off every aspect of feminine existence, trashing the roles of wives and mothers. She simply wanted laws that recognized women as fully legal, adult entities in this new nation. She was linking the cause of women—and at other times, the cause of abolition—to the cause of the Revolution. Though her husband did not take her seriously on this point, she remained faithful to her family, loving John and their children throughout fifty-four years of marriage. As one biographer noted, "In her eyes, improved legal and social status for women was not inconsistent with their essentially domestic role."[2]

Though Abigail Adams would not be considered a feminist, she did accurately predict the feminist rebellion to come. In her rightful plea, she also articulated what would become a basic feminist premise: *"Remember, all men would be tyrants if they could."*

Whenever women have considered our history of inequality, the consistent conclusion has been that men are the problem. In this chapter, we'll explore how feminism developed around this idea and how the Bible addresses this tension between the sexes. This is some of the history about women and feminism that I learned well after my women's studies courses—history that has been eye-opening to learn.

Pursuing Rights

The preamble to the Declaration of Independence holds one of the most memorable sentences in American history: "We hold these truths to be self-evident, that all men are created equal, that they are endowed by their Creator with certain unalienable Rights, that among these are Life, Liberty and the pursuit of Happiness." But in 1776, "all men" did not actually mean all men. It excluded some men—most notably, slaves—and all women.

The door to change, however, had been cracked open. Succeeding generations of women continued where Abigail Adams left off. In 1848, the Seneca Falls Women's Rights Convention assembled in Seneca Falls, New York. The convention was convened by five women, including activists Elizabeth Cady Stanton and Lucretia Mott. The participants issued a Declaration of Sentiments, modeled after the Declaration of Independence, which called for equal treatment of women under the law.

Historians today generally pinpoint this nineteenth-century convention as the inception of the feminist movement. It is considered the starting point of the first wave of feminism, also known as the suffrage movement or the campaign to obtain women's right to vote. That campaign took some time too—women were finally granted the right to vote with the ratification of the Nineteenth Amendment to the Constitution in 1920. That's about as much as most people know about the first wave of feminism, if indeed they are aware there have been multiple waves. I didn't learn this even in my women's studies courses, so I don't expect it is common knowledge.

As important as it was to these early feminists to obtain the right to vote, two additional issues were just as significant: coverture and the reform of Christianity. Coverture was the legal concept that subordinated a woman's property rights in marriage. Prior to marriage at that time, a woman could freely execute a will, enter into contracts, sue or be sued in her own name, and sell or give away her real estate or personal property as she wished. Upon marriage, however, her individual legal identity and existence was suspended. This was among the grievances the Seneca Falls organizers addressed in the Declaration of Sentiments, which they termed "a history of repeated injuries and usurpations on the part of man toward woman."

- He has never permitted her to exercise her inalienable right to the elective franchise.
- He has compelled her to submit to laws, in the formation of which she had no voice.
- He has withheld from her rights which are given to the most ignorant and degraded men—both natives and foreigners.
- He has made her, if married, in the eye of the law, civilly dead.

- He has taken from her all right in property, even to the wages she earns.
- After depriving her of all rights as a married woman, if single and the owner of property, he has taxed her to support a government which recognizes her only when her property can be made profitable to it.
- He has monopolized nearly all the profitable employments, and from those she is permitted to follow, she receives but a scanty remuneration.
- He has denied her the facilities for obtaining a thorough education—all colleges being closed against her.[3]

The Seneca Falls organizers also addressed the church, which may seem surprising in our secular age, and issued a resolution for change:

He allows her in church, as well as state, but a subordinate position, claiming apostolic authority for her exclusion from the ministry, and, with some exceptions, from any public participation in the affairs of the church. . . . Resolved, that woman has too long rested satisfied in the circumscribed limits which corrupt customs and a perverted application of the Scriptures have marked out for her, and that it is time she should move in the enlarged sphere which her great Creator has assigned her.[4]

Even for these activists with all their outrage, it was still a bold maneuver to sign the document:

A crowd of about three hundred people, including forty men, came from five miles round. No woman felt capable of presiding; the task was undertaken by Lucretia's husband, James Mott. All of the resolutions were passed unanimously except for woman suffrage, a strange idea and scarcely a concept designed to appeal to the predominantly Quaker audience, whose male contingent commonly declined to vote. The eloquent Frederick Douglass, a former slave and now editor of the Rochester North Star, however, swayed the gathering into agreeing to the resolution. At the closing session, Lucretia Mott won approval of a final resolve "for the overthrowing of the monopoly of the pulpit, and for the securing to woman equal participation with men in the various trades, professions and commerce." One hundred women and men signed the Seneca Falls Declaration—although subsequent criticism caused some of them to remove their names.[5]

The challenge in reviewing history is to understand the tenor of the times and then to be able to objectively separate certain events to examine their future impact. In the case of the Declaration of Sentiments, we who are alive today have much for which to be thankful. These grievances led to needed reforms in education, marriage, suffrage, and employment for women. But mixed in with those needed social reforms was a challenge to Christianity—its church governance, biblical teaching, and community service. As we will see in chapter 8, the church in general needed a better understanding of a New Testament–based spiritual community. However, the challenge to the church that was raised in this document eventually led to the destruction of biblically defined concepts of God, sin, gender differences, marriage, and more.

To understand how this came about, each chapter in this book will address different aspects of feminism's influence, including marriage, motherhood, and female sexuality. In this chapter, I profile three leading feminists—Elizabeth Cady Stanton, Simone de Beauvoir, and Betty Friedan—to focus on their attitudes toward men and how those ideas contributed to the rise of feminism.

"In Silence and Subjection"

In many ways, Elizabeth Cady Stanton was the embodiment of first-wave feminism. The Seneca Falls Convention was the beginning of her lifelong crusade. Though Stanton was married for nearly fifty years and was the mother of seven children, she had a dim view of the institution of marriage: "It is in vain to look for the elevation of woman, so long as she is degraded in marriage. . . . I feel that this whole question of woman's rights turns on the point of the marriage relation."[6]

To be fair, her view of marriage may have been soured by the thoughtlessness of her own husband, Henry Stanton. She often confided her woes to her close friend and fellow activist, a single woman named Susan B. Anthony. In one letter, she wrote: "I pace up and down these two chambers of mine like a caged lion, longing to bring to a close childrearing and housekeeping cares. I have other work at hand." And again: "Oh, how I long for a few hours of leisure each day. How rebellious it makes me feel when I see Henry going about where and when and how he pleases. He can walk at will through the whole wide world or shut himself up alone, if he pleases, within four walls. As I contrast his freedom with my bondage, and feel that because of the false position of women, I have been compelled to hold all my noblest aspirations in abeyance in order to be a wife, a mother, a nurse, a cook, a household drudge, I am fired anew and long to pour forth from my own experience the whole long story of woman's wrongs."[7]

Her activism started with marriage reform and suffrage and then migrated to religion. Stanton developed her atheistic beliefs as a young woman in reaction to the revival meetings of evangelist Charles Finney. After hearing Finney preach, Stanton was terrified of damnation: "Fear of judgment seized my soul. Visions of the lost haunted my dreams. Mental anguish prostrated my health. Dethronement of my reason was apprehended by my friends. . . . Returning at night, I often at night roused my father from his slumbers to pray for me, lest I should be cast into the bottomless pit before morning."[8]

But this conviction did not last long. Her family convinced her to ignore Finney's preaching and took her away on holiday to Niagara Falls in order to clear her mind. Following this vacation, she wrote:

> Thus, after many months of weary wandering in the intellectual labyrinth of "The Fall of Man," "Original Sin," "Total Depravity," "God's Wrath," "Satan's Triumph," "The Crucifixion," "The Atonement," and "Salvation by Faith," I found my way out of the darkness into the clear sunlight of Truth. My religious superstitions gave place to rational ideas based on scientific facts, and in proportion, as I looked at everything from a new standpoint, I grew more and more happy, day by day. . . . I view it as one of the greatest crimes to shadow the minds of the young with these gloomy superstitions; and with fears of the unknown and the unknowable to poison all their joy in life.[9]

Her bias against Christianity only grew stronger with time. Toward the end of her life, Stanton published *The Woman's Bible*, a feminist recasting of the Scriptures. In the introduction, she wrote:

> The Bible teaches that woman brought sin and death into the world, that she precipitated the fall of the race, that she was arraigned before the judgment seat of Heaven, tried, condemned and sentenced. Marriage for her was to be a condition of bondage, maternity a period of suffering and anguish, and in silence and subjection, she was to play the role of a dependent on man's bounty for all her material wants, and for all the information she might desire on the vital questions of the hour, she was commanded to ask her husband at home. Here is the Bible position of woman briefly summed up.[10]

The irony of Stanton's claims is that when the Bible is actually properly taught, history shows that women's status improves. The Protestant Reformation several hundred years earlier had *positively* affected the status of wives as marriage came under the rallying cry of *sola Scriptura* (Latin for "by Scripture alone"). Even secular historians concede that few people shaped the institution of marriage more than Martin Luther. His opposition to the mandatory celibacy of priests led to his well-articulated positions on marriage, and ultimately to his own marriage in 1525. At forty-two, this former monk married a twenty-five-year-old former nun, and together they became parents to six children. As Luther and other Protestants examined the Scriptures, they exalted "companionate marriage," over and against the traditional financial gains and political alliances sought through marriage.

In her book, *A History of the Wife*, Marilyn Yalom provides this summary of the Protestant legacy:

> Returning to the words of Genesis, English Protestants took very seriously God's statement, "It is not good for the man to be alone" and that a wife was to be "a sustainer beside him." Hand in hand, two Christian souls were encouraged to share the pleasures and duties of this earth as they simultaneously made their own way, step by step, to eternal life. And among the pleasures that Protestants recognized and condoned were the pleasures of marital sex. Puritans, in particular,

contrary to the now popular view of them as inhibited hypocrites, saw regular sexual intercourse as necessary for a lasting marriage. . . .[11]

As we look back on this period from the vantage of the year 2000, it can be argued that sixteenth- and seventeenth-century Protestants prepared the soil for modern marriage. The American historian Edmund Morgan reminds us of the high value placed on mutual love in Puritan marriage: "If the husband and wife failed to love each other above all the world, they not only wronged each other they disobeyed God."[12]

So as you can see, while the crowning achievements of the first-wave feminist movement were the legal reforms of coverture and suffrage, Stanton's writings reveal the ongoing target was the authority of Scripture. This is still true today.

After the ratification of the Nineteenth Amendment in 1920, feminism as an activist movement in the United States seemed to fade away. In my opinion, that was due more to the distractions of World Wars I and II and the Great Depression. But in Europe, where feminism was more directly linked to the socialist movement, it continued to percolate—especially in the "café culture" of Paris, the place where the woman credited with the rise of feminism's second wave and her lover were often found.

The Second Sex

Jean-Paul Sartre was a leading intellectual, a man who published the philosophical treatises he wrote while sitting among like-minded friends in French cafés. Simone de Beauvoir was his equal professionally and intellectually (they took the two top honors in philosophy at the Sorbonne). In some circles, Sartre and Beauvoir are still considered one of the most influential couples of the twentieth century. Their political cause, socialism, has sputtered to near irrelevance, but their influence on modern marriage remains indelible.

Sartre and Beauvoir met in 1929, when she was twenty-one and he was twenty-four, and they decided upon a radical relationship. Forsaking the "confines of bourgeoisie marriage," they defined their lifelong union as an open relationship, a nonmonogamous, nonmarital union that only required "complete transparency":

Sartre felt strongly that love was not about possession. To him, a more generous kind of love was to love the other person as a free being. When Beauvoir raised the thorny question of jealousy, Sartre said that if they told each other everything, they would never feel excluded from each other's lives. . . . While Sartre did not want to lose a freedom he had already enjoyed for several years, Beauvoir could not even quite imagine what her freedom would look like. . . . "I had not emancipated myself from all sexual taboos," she admits. "Promiscuity in a woman still shocked me."[13]

As matters worked out, the pact meant that Beauvoir not only discussed with Sartre his interest in other women; she often formed intimate friendships with the women herself. . . . Sartre soon stopped sleeping with her, and she had her own serious affairs. . . . But she remained committed to Sartre and to the pact; and the relationship, with its carrousel of changing partners and café tables, lasted fifty-one years.[14]

Beauvoir was best known for the 1949 French publication *Le Deuxième Sexe* (*The Second Sex*), her comprehensive study of the secondary status of women throughout history. As the first full-length socio-philosophical examination of the status of women in society, *The Second Sex* is said to be the seminal work of modern feminism. Beauvoir wrote that woman "is defined and differentiated with reference to man and not he with reference to her; she is the incidental, the inessential as opposed to the essential. He is the Subject, he is the Absolute—she is the Other."[15] Because of this secondary status, Beauvoir argued that women were "imprisoned" by the roles of wife, mother, and sweetheart; therefore, she maintained that "all forms of socialism, wresting woman away from the family, favor her liberation."[16]

However, when her own life is examined, Beauvoir is a paradoxical feminist. She was a lifelong partner to a man who compulsively seduced numerous women. Worse yet, she herself was part of his predatory relationships with young women—one who suffered a nervous breakdown, two who committed suicide, and a fourth who endured three abortions to "spare" Sartre the burden of fatherhood.[17] Their private correspondence, published after their deaths in the 1980s, revealed jealousies, boorish behavior, lies, and contempt for those they seduced—which stunned and angered those intimates who were still alive. According to a recent profile in the *New Yorker*, those letters also put Beauvoir's views of marriage and male-female relations to the test:

> If "The Second Sex" can't be squared with the life, we are reduced to the final, depressing theory that the pact was just the traditional sexist arrangement—in which the man sleeps around and the woman nobly "accepts" the situation—on philosophical stilts. Sartre was the classic womanizer, and Beauvoir was the classic enabler. . . . Beauvoir was formidable, but she was not made of ice. Though her affairs, for the most part, were love affairs, it is plain from almost every page she wrote that she would have given them all up if she could have had Sartre for herself alone.[18]

In *The Second Sex*, Beauvoir wrote that "all male ideologies are directed at justifying the oppression of women . . . women are so conditioned by society that they consent to this oppression."[19] With the perspective of hindsight, it would seem that the woman who claimed other women were imprisoned within the roles of wife, mother, and sweetheart lived in sordid bondage herself. Ironically, toward the end of her life, she said that nothing she achieved in her professional life was as great as her relationship with Sartre.

He died in 1980, cutting her out of his will and leaving his estate to his final mistress.[20]

Sartre and Beauvoir were champions of existentialism, a philosophy that can be loosely defined as a system in which subjectivity, individual freedom, and choice are championed—"truth that is true for me," as one existentialist philosopher wrote.[21] Their relationship was one widely emulated by the postwar generation, the Baby Boomers who claimed that they, too, did not need "a piece of paper" to confirm their relationships.

The Problem That Has No Name

The Second Sex was published in English in 1953, but it wasn't widely read in the United States until after Betty Friedan echoed it in her 1963 publication, *The Feminine Mystique*. In the book, Friedan explores a "nameless, aching dissatisfaction" among suburban housewives that she would term "the problem that has no name." Her theory was that women were trying to live up to a feminine ideal (the "mystique") that left them feeling trapped, bored, and depressed. She wrote:

> The suburban housewife—she was the dream image of the young American women and the envy, it was said, of women all over the world. The American housewife—freed by science and labor-saving appliances from the drudgery, the dangers of childbirth and the illnesses of her grandmother. She was healthy, beautiful, educated, concerned only about her husband, her children, her home. She had found true feminine fulfillment. As a housewife and mother, she was respected as a full and equal partner to man in his world. She was free to choose automobiles, clothes, appliances, supermarkets; she had everything that women ever dreamed of. In the fifteen years after World War II, this mystique of feminine fulfillment became the cherished and self-perpetuating core of contemporary American culture.[22]

When you consider the history of feminism, Friedan's words are somewhat amusing. Two hundred years earlier, Abigail Adams was asking her husband to grant full rights to the female citizens of this new nation—a serious request. And one hundred years earlier, women like Elizabeth Cady Stanton were organizing for women's suffrage and the reform of marriage laws—again, grave impediments. But now Friedan was addressing feminine *boredom* amid all the consumer goods! (I'm sure there are impoverished women in developing nations everywhere who would like to have such problems.) Ultmately, Friedan defined the "problem that has no name" as the "voice within women that says: 'I want something more than my husband and my children and my home.'"[23]

Friedan decided activism would solve the problem, so she went on to cofound the National Organization for Women (NOW) and served as its first president from 1966 to 1970. She was also a cofounder of NARAL, the pro-abortion political action group, and the National Women's Political Caucus. But her activism came with a cost. Characterizing her marriage as one based not "on love but on dependent hate," Friedan concluded that she could no longer continue "leading other women out of the wilderness while holding on to a marriage that destroyed my self-respect."[24] She divorced her husband, Carl, in 1969.

In her memoir *Life So Far*, published in 2000, she claimed Carl had beaten her during their marriage, a charge she later softened in media interviews.[25] Outraged, her former husband set up a website to refute her charges. He wrote, "I have not lived eighty years of an honorable life to have it trashed by a mad woman . . . I have been divorced from her for thirty years and still she haunts me and disrupts my life."[26] Though he continued to identify himself as a feminist, Carl said, "I would just advise a person not to marry one."[27]

Despite this turmoil and the way she vilified marriage as a younger feminist, Friedan modified her perspective later in life. In the posthumous tribute published by the *Christian Science Monitor*, Friedan's support for marriage was evident:

> Her commanding, sometimes brusque, public persona gave little hint of the softer, private Friedan who expressed pride in her three children and nine grandchildren. Ever the doting grandmother, Friedan the adventurer planned to take each one on a trip. One year she and her oldest grandson traveled to Cuba. Later she and another grandson went hot-air ballooning in France.
>
> She called the failure of her own marriage "perhaps my main regret" in a Monitor interview. "I believe in marriage. I think intimacy, bonding, and families have value." Expressing the hope that her grandchildren would marry and have children, she said, "Families are a great thing."[28]

When she died in 2006, Friedan was lionized by the *Washington Post* "as the feminist crusader and author whose searing first book, 'The Feminine Mystique,' ignited the contemporary women's movement in 1963 and as a result permanently transformed the social fabric of the United States and countries around the world."[29]

Friedan will always be linked with feminism's second wave—a movement generally seen as cresting in the 1970s and washing out by the mid-1980s. A third wave—not as well-documented in mainstream press—arose in the early 1990s as a reaction to what was perceived as the upper-middle class, white woman's orientation of the second wave. Harder to document as a movement, the influence of the third wave can best be seen in pop culture—the early influence of the "riot grrrl" bands, the buff and barely dressed video vixens, and the raunch culture evidenced in tweeners wearing Playboy Bunny shirts and suburban gyms offering pole-dancing aerobics. We'll further examine third-wave feminism in chapter 7.

The Lens of Wisdom

The lives of Stanton, Beauvoir, and Friedan span all three waves of feminism. Yet their relationships with men were the cause of either profound regret or posthumous repugnance. These fiery and articulate women commanded a lot of attention for their ideas. But how are we to judge their legacies?

The apostle James hands us this clear-eyed and reasonable method of evaluation:

> *Who is wise and understanding among you? By his good conduct let him show his works in the meekness of wisdom. But if you have bitter jealousy and selfish ambition in your hearts, do not boast and be false to the truth. This is not the wisdom that comes down from above, but is earthly, unspiritual, demonic. For where jealousy and selfish ambition exist, there will be disorder and every vile practice. But the wisdom from above is first pure, then peaceable, gentle, open to reason, full of mercy and good fruits, impartial and sincere. And a harvest of righteousness is sown in peace by those who make peace.* (James 3:13–18)

Jealousy, selfish ambition, disorder, and every vile practice characterize false wisdom. But purity, peace, gentleness, right thinking, and mercy—virtues that lead to a harvest of good fruit and righteousness in the lives of those who pursue such wisdom—characterize the wisdom of heaven. As the old adage goes, right thinking leads to right living. Hopefully, this has been and will continue to be evident in all of the personal stories presented in this book. But if "right living" is our only plumb line, we will soon discover no one measures up completely. It's unwise to compare ourselves to each other. Human experience can't be our standard because it's flawed and incomplete. In order to possess the "good fruits" listed above, we need to consider their source—God.

Beauvoir, Friedan, and Stanton were bright, articulate women. Presumably, they were good at observing situations and describing them. But were they correctly *comprehending* their situations? Beauvoir expended great effort to categorize the male-female dynamic, concluding that women have been held in a relationship of long-standing oppression by men through their relegation to being men's "Other." But in her analysis, Beauvoir missed the *real* Absolute, the true Subject: God. We—men and women alike—are all the Other in relation to the One who created us. *God* is essential. We are the incidental and inessential ones. History is not the story of our puny accomplishments. It is the story of God's redemptive activity in and among us.

Redemptive—I used that word on purpose because it highlights the true problem. There is real tension between the Absolute and the Other. The reason is sin. Our sinful actions, thoughts, attitudes, and words are the reason for the chasm between God and human beings. Sin also separates us from one another. We need to be *redeemed* from the consequences of sin—God's righteous judgment and wrath—to experience true freedom. Being male and female is not the problem. In fact, when God created man and woman, He called it very good.

> *Then God said, "Let us make man in our image, after our likeness. And let them have dominion over the fish of the sea and over the birds of the heavens and over the livestock and over all the earth and over every creeping thing that creeps on the earth." So God created man in his own image, in the image of God he created him; male and female he created them. . . . And God saw everything that he had made, and behold, it was very good. And there was evening and there was morning, the sixth day.* (Genesis 1:26–27, 31, emphasis mine)

Masculinity and femininity are God's idea and creation. There is something that reflects God in each sex. So men as a gender class are not the problem, biblically speaking. The *real* problem is that a man once stood by his wife as she listened to God's enemy question His authority, His goodness, and His boundaries. The man did not intervene in any way. Instead, he was a monument to passivity. His only action was to eat the forbidden fruit his wife gave to him. For her part, the woman knew the life-preserving boundaries the Lord God had established, but in her quest to be like God, she violated those boundaries, sinfully judged God's motives and orders, and gave in to her own assessment of the situation. What she clapped her eyes upon, she desired. Circumventing authority, she grasped for something that had not been given to her, and her husband went right along with her.

> Now the serpent was more crafty than any of the wild animals the Lord God had made. He said to the woman, "Did God really say, 'You must not eat from any tree in the garden'?" The woman said to the serpent, "We may eat fruit from the trees in the garden, but God did say, 'You must not eat fruit from the tree that is in the middle of the garden, and you must not touch it, or you will die.'" "You will not surely die," the serpent said to the woman. "For God knows that when you eat of it your eyes will be opened, and you will be like God, knowing good and evil." When the woman saw that the fruit of the tree was good for food and pleasing to the eye, and also desirable for gaining wisdom, she took some and ate it. She also gave some to her husband, who was with her, and he ate it. (Genesis 3:1–6 NIV)

The result of this momentous decision is the world you and I live in—a world fueled by selfishness, pride, and anger that results in conflict, death, and decay. When Adam and Eve sinned, they forfeited life in the goodness of the garden of Eden. They traded unhindered fellowship with God for the curses of marital strife, painful childbirth, futile toil, death, and most importantly, separation from God. They were the first ones to sin, but we are no different.

This passage teaches us that women do have a problem. But it's not men. It's *sin*. Sin warps everything, including the good that God has designed in being a man or a woman. Women sin against men and men sin against women, and everyone sins against God and falls short of His standard of holiness and perfection. Sin is the reason men have oppressed women and women have usurped men. Sin is the reason for the jealousy, selfish ambition, disorder, and every vile practice that characterizes false wisdom. Sin is the reason we need a Savior.

When Abigail Adams wrote "all men would be tyrants if they could," her words were likely a mix of sinful judgment on her part ("*all* men") and an accurate understanding of sin in general. As a movement, feminism arose because women were being sinned against. I think that is a fair argument. But feminism also arose because women were sinning in response. That's a classic human problem: Sinners tend to sin in response to being sinned against.

The glorious hope we have is that Christ came to rescue us from this spiral of sin and sinful response. Only the gospel can accurately diagnose the issues on both sides and offer both the good news of forgiveness for our sins and the restoration of our relationship first with God and then with each other.

This is true liberation for women . . . and men.

"MEN ARE SCUM"

IN THE PREVIOUS CHAPTER, we encountered the stories of leading feminists who blamed men for their problems. Here is the story of my friend Emma, who had many reasons to distrust men and yet, through the gospel, she was able to respond differently. You may be in a similar situation and wondering how you can apply the "wisdom from above" that is peaceable and merciful (James 3:13–18). I hope that Emma's story will encourage you that God's grace is no mere concept but is a powerful force for real change.

Emma could hear the bickering start in the adjacent room. She plugged her ears, attempting to block the sound of anger. It was always difficult to endure. But this time, in the concert of conflict, one note sounded different—it was fear. Emma recognized her mother was in real danger.

Pushing open her parents' bedroom door, she saw her mother staring at her father as he cocked his rifle at her. Sizing up the situation, Emma took a bold step for a petite fourteen-year-old girl. She ran in between her parents, pushed her mother away, and began yelling for her mother to leave the room. Adrenaline surged through her, overriding all her fears.

Her father put the gun down, shouting for her to get out of the room.

Though she had never seen her father pull a gun on her mother, Emma wasn't surprised he would do it—even in a new country in a quiet suburban neighborhood. That was how he had begun their marriage decades ago in Jordan. At twenty-five, he had decided he wanted to marry his younger cousin. So he kidnapped her from school one day, loading her into a car at gunpoint. He escaped in a barrage of gunfire and married her immediately afterward. Though Emma's grandmother had tried to rescue her daughter, for reasons unfathomable to all, Emma's mother refused to leave her husband.

Shortly after the rifle incident, Emma announced to her mother that she would never get married because "all men are scum." Her mother rebuked her, saying not all men are like that. So Emma challenged her to name one happily married couple.

After a long silence, her mother looked at her sadly and conceded the point.

"I grew up in a situation where every man I knew from among my own family and friends was not trustworthy," Emma recalls. "The conclusion I came to was that men were no good—they were bums. My mom was the strong one in the family. Were it not for my mom, financially we wouldn't have made it. Without her, we wouldn't have had food to eat or a house to live in. My dad liked to appear that he wore the pants in the family, but my mom was the backbone. She made sure the money came in. She even ran his own business while he watched TV in the back room."

Emma was ten when her family emigrated from Jordan to the United States. She had grown up in a nominally religious family, but she didn't know much about her own religion (which has its roots in an Islamic sect). During her first summer in the United States, Emma met a lifeguard at the apartment complex pool, a young woman who talked about Jesus Christ to the group of young children who were always hanging around. Emma had never heard of Jesus before. Fascinated, she began to arrive early to help clean the pool and conduct a Bible study with the lifeguard.

When they found out about this, Emma's parents were livid. They were mad at the lifeguard, convinced that their daughter was being brainwashed. They threatened Emma with going back to live in Jordan with her grandmother. But Emma was steadfast in her commitment.

"They were trying to tell me about their god, so I said, 'If your god was real, you would have told me about it earlier,'" she says. "You don't proselytize people into my family's religion—you are born into it and that's it. That's why to leave the faith or to marry someone outside of this faith is scandalous."

Her faith was what emboldened her to take action the day Emma confronted her father with the rifle. "I looked him in the eye and said, 'Daddy, I am not afraid to die.' All I knew then was that I was a believer and he was not, so I refused to be intimidated," she recalls.

Emma persevered in her faith, and she even convinced her parents to allow her to attend a Christian college. In her junior year, she met a young man named Chase Davidson. They quickly became friends, but she did not allow him to cross the line into dating. Their friendship grew for several years until Emma left for graduate school to study counseling. She had grown quite fond of Chase by then, even to the point of trusting him, so their close friendship confused her.

Emma threw herself into her studies and began to work on rape trauma and sexual abuse cases. Unfortunately, that casework only strengthened her negative view of men. Mercifully, she began to attend a church near her school where her prejudices and the gaps in her Christian doctrine were corrected.

"At this point, I desperately needed a biblical framework for all the sin I was seeing," Emma says. "It wasn't just my sisters or my girlfriends getting their hearts broken by unfaithful boyfriends. It wasn't just my father being abusive and lazy or my brother's promiscuity. Now I was dealing with children who had been sexually abused and women who had been raped. I was increasingly distrustful, so it was God's kind providence to lead me to a church where I was being instructed biblically. Even though I had been a Christian since I was ten, I didn't have the complete picture. Up until that point, I had always been in churches where the women had strong personalities and the men were either absent or passive. I hadn't seen men lead without sinfully dominating their families."

As Emma began to babysit for her pastor's family, she was able to see how her pastor lived what he taught and how he cared for his family. She joined a small group at her church, where she became good friends with many married couples and saw marriages that were healthy and God-honoring. Eventually she had faith for getting married herself. Emma and Chase were married less than two years later. Now they have three children, and Emma trains women in her church to counsel other women who are victims of abuse or trauma.

"It's one thing to observe and describe a problem; it's another thing to interpret a problem," Emma says. "Many people can be very good at describing a problem and labeling a set of behaviors. But where they can go wrong is in understanding the root issues of a problem. Our problem is our fallen nature. It's about sin. We need to know our bent that necessitated the cross of Christ. I thank God that I began to go to a church where biblical foundations were being laid at the same time I was starting work on these abuse cases. Having all of that information minus a file system to categorize it—that biblical framework—would have been very hard, even dangerous, for me."

Emma's father died last year. She spent the last several months of his life caring for him as cancer sapped his life from him. She prayed for him constantly and also made sure he heard the gospel several times before he passed away. He wasn't as resistant to the gospel by the time he died, but she remains unsure of his spiritual status. Nevertheless, she considers it a victory in Christ that she was able to forgive him and help care for him until his final hour on earth.

That peacemaking mercy is the fruit of the wisdom that comes from above.

Three

"DID GOD
Really Say . . . ?"

f you claim men are women's chief problem, it has a way of
dissuading women from marrying men . . . and vice versa.
Therefore, it's no surprise that feminism profoundly affected marriage
rates and longevity—not to mention the definition of marriage. If you
are a young woman, you may find that few of your non-Christian peers
are truly planning on marriage. If you are a little older, you may be seeing a wave of divorces among your friends, many of which are initiated by women. There's a reason for these trends—reasons we will
explore in this and the following chapter.

Though we do look at a few feminist perspectives on marriage in
the following pages, I think it's more important to spend some time
examining what God's Word says about marriage, especially about
that provocative topic of submission. You may be pleasantly surprised that the Bible's definition challenges your assumptions. The
most important thing for every woman to note—married or not—is
that a war is going on. But it's not the classic war of the sexes. It's far
more serious.

FOR MANY AMERICANS in the early 1970s, the face of feminism was that of Gloria Steinem. An attractive woman with long blonde hair and a penchant for delivering pithy one-liners, she became a telegenic spokeswoman for the movement. As a professional journalist, Steinem used her skills and experience to found the feminist magazine *Ms.* in 1971 and to cofound the National Women's Political Caucus in 1972.

Marriage was often the subject of her memorable quotes:

- "Some of us are becoming the men we wanted to marry."
- "A liberated woman is one who has sex before marriage and a job after."
- "I can't mate in captivity."
- "Someone asked me why women don't gamble as much as men do, and I gave the commonsensical reply that we don't have as much money. That was a true and incomplete answer. In fact, women's total instinct for gambling is satisfied by marriage."[1]
- "Marriage is designed for a person-and-a-half."[2]
- "The surest way to be alone is to get married."[3]
- "A woman needs a man like a fish needs a bicycle." (A line Gloria Steinem made famous, quoting Australian feminist Irina Dunn.)[4]

So when Steinem wed for the first time at age sixty-six, she caught fellow activists off guard. Steinem and South African businessman David Bale were married in Oklahoma at the home of Steinem's close friend, Wilma Mankiller, the first female chief of the Cherokee Nation. Sadly, Steinem and Bale were married for only three years before he died of brain lymphoma at age sixty-two.

Before her husband died, Steinem told the *Washington Post* why her attitude toward marriage had changed over the past thirty years:

If I had gotten married when I was supposed to, I would have lost most of my civil rights—my name, my credit rating, my legal residence, my ability to get a loan or start a business. Socially as well as legally, a married couple was one person and that person was the man. The women's movement has fought for thirty years to change those laws, so that now an equal partnership in marriage is possible—still not socially easy, but possible. So my attitude towards marriage has changed as marriage has changed.

I agree with you that we should be free to choose or not choose marriage, and the big remaining barrier to that freedom of choice is the inability of two women or two men to marry. That's because the state still says that marriage is about reproduction, even though a man and women [*sic*] can marry and choose not to reproduce. For myself personally, I didn't see the motivation or difference between living together and being married until I realized that the man I was in love with and I would not have the ability to, for instance, make a health decision for the other one if one of us was incapacitated. We wanted a commitment to each other, equal marriage is now legally possible, and so we did marry. It made me realize more deeply the unfairness of closing this choice to some and not others.[5]

In that statement, Steinem updated herself, combining both second-wave and third-wave feminist attitudes toward marriage. When Steinem launched *Ms.* magazine in the early 1970s, the conversation about marriage and family was generally framed by the conventional heterosexual, nuclear-family model. By the time she got married, third-wave feminists were not just trying to reform an institution; they were looking to alter it beyond recognition.

Take, for example, Jennifer Baumgardner and Amy Richards, daughters of second-wave feminists who eventually became editors at *Ms.* magazine in the early 1990s. They are the authors of a leading third-wave feminist book, *Manifesta: Young Women, Feminism, and the Future.* When asked about marriage a few years ago, Richards outlined the third wave's goals of first eliminating the institution of marriage and then eliminating biology from the definition of family:

I think that marriage first has to be available to all—same sex couples— and the respect of marriage has to be afforded to committed relationships before we can consider eliminating marriage. I think the family should not be eliminated but redefined. We have done a good job of "adding" to family—making it about "more than biology"—

however, we haven't yet eliminated biology from that definition and, personally, I think that family should be an emotional bond, not a biological one. Hopefully we will begin to consider this in greater detail as more people use technology to have children.[6]

One of my goals in writing this book was to avoid the shrill verbiage of political talk shows—the us-versus-them polemic that paints everything in extremes. But in mere print that can be hard to avoid when the worldviews are so radically different between feminism and Christian faith. This quote from *Manifesta* sums it up well:

> Feminism is more often described by what it isn't than by what it is, which creates some confusion (and this is the reason that we defined it before going into all this). The inadvertently humorous descriptions by right-wing ideologues like Pat Robertson don't help, either: "Feminists encourage women to leave their husbands, kill their children, practice witchcraft, become lesbians, and destroy capitalism." Of course, that definition is not so much wrong as hyperbolic. To a fundamentalist, that's just a description of no-fault divorce laws, abortion rights, rejection of God as the Father, acceptance of female sexuality, and a commitment to workers.[7]

While I rarely find myself in agreement with either Pat Robertson or Jennifer Baumgardner and Amy Richards, this quote does nail the true problem: rejection of God as the Father. As Steinem said in a 2005 interview, "Monotheism makes me grouchy. I don't trust any religion that makes God look like one of the ruling class. I guess I'm a pagan or an animist."[8]

God's authority in creating and defining marriage is what is on trial with feminism. Therefore, in this chapter we will explore what the Bible says about the institution of marriage.

A Spiritual Crisis

I would bet that if you asked most people what's happened to the institution of marriage, the answer you would receive would likely revolve around the high rate of divorce. Or perhaps you might hear about the growing number of domestic partnerships. These are the stories the mainstream media tracks. For example, in early 2007 the *New York Times* announced that more American women were living without a husband than with one. The newspaper cited statistics that in 2005, 51 percent of women said they were living without a spouse, up from 49 percent in 2000 and 35 percent in 1950.[9]

The blogosphere lit up in reaction to this report, discussing the demise of marriage. The only problem? The story was eventually proven to be wrong. The reporter's analysis included teen girls between the ages of fifteen and nineteen (the vast majority of whom are unmarried at this stage of life) and excluded women who indicated they were married with an absent spouse (such as those with spouses in the military or in prison). The statistical analysis was believable to many, however, because of the intense cultural assault on marriage spanning the past forty years.

Whether you are single, married, divorced, or widowed, your relationships have been profoundly affected by feminism. It's not just that a few laws were revised regarding marriage, as Steinem stated. The fallout from feminism can be seen in the HPV vaccine your preteen daughter's school board insists she have right now to the gift registry your coworker announced because her boyfriend just moved in with her. There's nothing wrong with vaccines or gifts, but the underlying assumption is that marriage and sexual fidelity no longer matter. Like the Bible says in Judges 21:25, when there is no king—no ultimate authority—everyone does what is right in his or her own eyes. Though our culture has discarded the idea of God and His absolute authority, that hardly gets Him out of the picture. In fact, the hubris of creatures trying to oust their Creator only *highlights* the real problem.

Let me show you what I mean. There's a thick book that sits on my shelf that is an exhaustive study written by a seminary professor on all that the Bible has to say about marriage and family—titled, appropriately enough, *God, Marriage, and Family,* by Andreas Köstenberger. His comments are so relevant to this discussion that I'm going to excerpt a few key paragraphs from across several sections of his book to provide a framework for this topic:

For the first time in its history, Western civilization is confronted with
the need to define the meaning of the terms "marriage" and "family." . . .
The current cultural crisis, however, is merely symptomatic of a deep-
seated spiritual crisis that continues to gnaw at the foundations of our
once-shared societal values. If God the Creator in fact, as the Bible
teaches, instituted marriage and the family, and if there is an evil being
called Satan who wages war against God's creative purposes in this
world, it should come as no surprise that the divine foundation of
these institutions has come under massive attack in recent years. Ultimately, we human beings, whether we realize it or not, are involved in
a cosmic spiritual conflict that pits God against Satan, with marriage
and the family serving as a key arena in which spiritual and cultural
battles are fought. If, then, the cultural crisis is symptomatic of an underlying spiritual crisis, the solution likewise must be spiritual, not
merely cultural.[10]

Feminism is a contemporary manifestation of this timeless spiritual battle. In past eras, other dominant sins—such as chauvinism and
polygamy—marred God's design for marriage and family. But today
it's important that we clearly understand that the change in our culture is evidence of a spiritual crisis more than a cultural crisis. I may
not agree with one bit of what Gloria Steinem says about marriage,
but she and other feminists are not my enemy. For Christians, our true
enemies are *spiritual*. "For we do not wrestle against flesh and blood,
but against the rulers, against the authorities, against the cosmic powers over this present darkness, against the spiritual forces of evil in the
heavenly places" (Ephesians 6:12).

The Bible teaches us that marriage is about much more than
having the legal ability to direct your spouse's health care or other
perceived civil rights. Its significance is greater than a big pageant on
your wedding day or all the stuff you can cram into your gift registry.
These are the concerns of finite human beings with finite perspectives.
Yes, it's rightful and necessary to have equal civil rights as a woman—
I certainly don't want to go back to the days without them! Gifts are
nice too. But seen in the big picture of Ephesians 6:12, these concerns
just don't matter much for those who live each day in the awareness
that there are spiritual forces that are arrayed against us.

So we are in a battle. But what does that look like? Are we supposed to walk around casting demons out of each others' marriages? Are we supposed to carry a sword on date nights? Actually, Köstenberger points out that we walk around *every day* with our most strategic weapon:

> What is the key element in spiritual warfare? According to Scripture, it is human minds. "But I am afraid that just as Eve was deceived by the serpent's cunning, your minds may somehow be led astray from your sincere and pure devotion to Christ" (2 Cor. 11:3 NIV). "For though we live in the world, we do not wage war as the world does. The weapons we fight with are not the weapons of the world. On the contrary, they have divine power to demolish strongholds. We demolish arguments and every pretension that sets itself up against the knowledge of God, and we take captive every thought to make it obedient to Christ" (10:3–5 NIV). Just as Satan reasoned with Eve as to why she should disobey God in the Garden, it is people's thought life that *is the arena in which our spiritual battles are won or lost.*[11]

I italicized that last line because it's important. We need to camp out for a moment on this momentous concept: *Spiritual battles are won or lost in the day-to-day thoughts we harbor.* Ideas matter! What we think about the purpose of marriage, the roles in marriage, and the priority of marriage *matters*, and it matters a great deal to God. Köstenberger continues:

> Spiritual warfare is the all-encompassing, ruling reality for the marital relationship. Those who ignore it do so at their own peril. Just as the devil attacks those with potential for church leadership, he seeks to subvert human marriages, because they have the greatest potential for displaying to the world the nature of the relationship between Christ and his church (Eph. 5:31–32).[12]

Do you see the spiritual battle in which we are *all* engaged? What each of us thinks and says about marriage is a part of that battle—whether we are presently married or not. *"Just as Satan reasoned with Eve as to why she should disobey God in the Garden, it is people's thought life that is the arena in which our spiritual battles are won or lost.*" Since the foundation of the world, Satan has been attacking our thinking about God's character and His intentions toward us. Eve knew that only *one* tree in the garden of Eden was off-limits to her and Adam, but Satan slithered in with an insinuation that God was holding out on her: "Did God really say, 'You must not eat from any tree in the garden'?" (Genesis 3:1 NIV).

The first question in the Bible comes from the Serpent twisting God's Word: "Did God really say . . . ?" And Eve's response is to add a further restriction to God's command: "We may eat fruit from the trees in the garden, but God did say, 'You must not eat fruit from the tree that is in the middle of the garden, and you must not touch it, or you will die'" (Genesis 3:2–3 NIV). God did not say Adam and Eve could not touch this tree, only that they may not eat from it.

As daughters of Eve, we need to realize the Serpent is still among us, asking the same question. "Did God really say . . . ?" You can fill in the blank with your own temptations and thoughts. You may hear questions buzzing around your head about God's definition of infidelity, motherhood, premarital sex, monogamy, the roles of men and women, the worth of a wife, the function of a family, and so on. These questions have a source—our spiritual Enemy—and an innate amplification system—our sinful hearts. And when the two mix, the results are combustible.

You see, the seeds of feminism lie within each of our hearts. Every one of us is prone to agree with Satan's character assassination of God. We often chafe at the good boundaries God has given us. We are easily tempted to think the worst of God. And we doubt that what God *has* provided is anywhere near as good as what He has restricted. In some ways, we have far more in common with self-proclaimed feminists than we may realize.

So let's look at an inflammatory issue in marriage: Did God *really* say that wives are to submit to their husbands?

Imitators of God

As I wrote in the first chapter of this book, the concept of submission was one of the first stumbling blocks I encountered as a new

Christian. I found this provoking verse about a wife's submission in the fifth chapter of Ephesians, a chapter that opens with these two verses:

> *Be imitators of God, therefore, as dearly loved children and live a life of love, just as Christ loved us and gave himself up for us as a fragrant offering and sacrifice to God.* (Ephesians 5:1–2 NIV)

Everything else that follows in this chapter—including that thorny submission verse—builds on the charge to live a life of love as an imitator of God. What many women overlook is that *submission is part of the divine character of the Trinity.* As theologian Wayne Grudem notes, the Bible frequently speaks of the differing roles and relationships within the Trinity:

> Never does Scripture say that the Son sends the Father into the world, or that the Holy Spirit sends the Father or the Son into the world, or that the Father obeys the commands of the Son or of the Holy Spirit. Never does Scripture say that the Son predestined us to be conformed to the image of the Father. The role of planning, directing, sending, and commanding the Son belongs to the Father only. . . .
>
> The Father has eternally had a leadership role, an authority to initiate and direct, that the Son does not have. Similarly, the Holy Spirit is subject to both the Father and the Son and plays yet a different role in Creation and in the work of salvation.
>
> When did the idea of headship and submission begin, then? The idea of headship and submission never began! It has always existed in the eternal nature of God Himself. And in this most basic of all authority relationships, authority is not based on gifts or ability (for the Father, Son, and Holy Spirit are equal in attributes and perfections). It is just there. Authority belongs to the Father, not because He is wiser or because He is a more skillful leader, but just because He is the Father.[13]

It's kind of hard to object to the concept of submission when you see it as a cornerstone of the Trinity, isn't it? The three divine persons of the Trinity are equal in nature, but different in role. *Feminists put a lot of emphasis on roles because they equate roles with inherent worth.* But that is not a biblical concept.

Right on the very first page of the Bible, we find an incredibly clear statement about the fundamental equality of men and women: "So God created man in his own image, in the image of God he created him; male and female he created them" (Genesis 1:27). This verse makes an extraordinary claim, according to Dr. Grudem:

> To be in the image of God is an incredible privilege. It means to be like God and to represent God. No other creatures in all of creation, not even the powerful angels, are said to be in the image of God. It is a privilege given only to us as men and women.
>
> Any discussion of manhood and womanhood in the Bible must start here. Every time we talk to each other as men and women, we should remember that the person we are talking to is a creature of God who is *more like God than anything else in the universe,* and men and women share that status equally. Therefore we should treat men and women with equal dignity and we should think of men and women as having equal value. We are *both* in the image of God, and we have been so since the first day that God created us. "In the image of God he created him; *male and female he created them*" (Genesis 1:27). Nowhere does the Bible say that men are more in God's image than women. Men and women share equally in the tremendous privilege of being in the image of God.
>
> The Bible thus corrects the errors of male dominance and male superiority that have come as the result of sin and that have been seen in nearly all cultures in the history of the world. Wherever men are thought to be better than women, wherever husbands act as selfish "dictators," wherever wives are forbidden to have their own jobs outside the home or to vote or to own property or to be educated, wherever women are treated as inferior, wherever there is abuse or violence against women or rape or female infanticide or polygamy or harems, the biblical truth of equality in the image of God is being denied. To all societies and cultures where these things occur, we must proclaim that the very first page of God's Word bears a fundamental and irrefutable witness against these evils.[14]

Amen! Isn't that powerfully encouraging? Despite our sinful human history of distorting God's Word, the Bible has *never* condoned these errors or actions.

However, as steeped as we are in our individualistic culture, we should note it is also a false assumption to conclude that each person reflects God in the *exact same way.* To accurately reflect God's image, we each would have to possess every one of His virtues—at least as much as flawed human beings can. But that doesn't seem possible even in natural observation. There are some people who reflect God's mercy better than others; there are some people who showcase God's creativity better than others; there are some people who manifest God's wisdom more than others, and so on. It is in our corporate witness that we most accurately reflect the manifold perfections of God. And the roles we inhabit are part of that corporate witness.

Live Wisely

Let's return to the progression of ideas in the fifth chapter of Ephesians. After exhorting us as dearly beloved children to be imitators of God and live a life of love, the apostle Paul describes what this looks like:

Be very careful, then, how you live—not as unwise but as wise, making the most of every opportunity, because the days are evil. Therefore do not be foolish, but understand what the Lord's will is. Do not get drunk on wine, which leads to debauchery. Instead, be filled with the Spirit. Speak to one another with psalms, hymns and spiritual songs. Sing and make music in your heart to the Lord, always giving thanks to God the Father for everything, in the name of our Lord Jesus Christ.

Submit to one another out of reverence for Christ.

Wives, submit to your husbands as to the Lord. For the husband is the head of the wife as Christ is the head of the church, his body, of which he is the Savior. Now as the church submits to Christ, so also wives should submit to their husbands in everything.

Husbands, love your wives, just as Christ loved the church and gave himself up for her to make her holy, cleansing her by the washing with water through the word, and to present her to himself as a radiant church, without stain or wrinkle or any other blemish, but holy and blameless. In this same way, husbands ought to love their wives as their own bodies. He who loves his wife loves himself. After all, no one ever hated his own body, but he feeds and cares for it, just as Christ does the church—for we are members of his body. "For this reason a man will leave his father and mother and be united to his wife, and the two will become one flesh." This is a profound mystery—but I am talking about Christ and the church. However, each one of you also must love his wife as he loves himself, and the wife must respect her husband. (Ephesians 5:15–33 NIV)

All of us are called to be very careful in how we live. All of us are called to live our lives in submission to Christ. We are to cultivate godly wisdom based on understanding what the Lord's will is. In the area of marriage, we need to know His will regarding this union and the roles within it. It is Christ's authority that rules over each of us, and in marriage both parties are submitted to Him. But there is a distinct way we acknowledge Christ's headship as either husbands or wives.

The first thing to note is the concise set of instructions to wives. This chapter contains many more verses directed to husbands than to wives, and they have the more difficult commands. Let's be honest: Submitting to and respecting a husband who leads and loves like Christ is the easier of the two roles! But in reality, no human husband ever perfectly fulfills those commands. That leaves a wife with the challenge of respecting and submitting to a flawed husband—a fact that surely didn't escape the Holy Spirit's notice when He inspired these verses.

The second thing to note is important: *Husbands* are not called to enforce submission. *Wives* are called to submit to their husbands because it's an expression of worship to the Lord. It is an act of love, freely offered. At the end of this passage, wives are also called to respect their husbands. The sense is that it is done out of their own volition. An alternate translation makes this point even clearer: "However, let each one of you love his wife as himself, and let the wife see that she respects her husband" (v. 33). The wife respects and submits to her husband *not* because his performance merits it, but because this is how she glorifies God in reflecting the mystery of Christ and the church.

This passage contradicts the feminist fear that complementary biblical roles are equivalent to sinful male domination of women. So when we find ourselves cringing at this verse—or awkwardly trying to explain it to non-Christian friends or family—it's good to remember four important things about this verse:

- Scripture does not call a woman to submit herself to all men, but only to one man—her husband.
- It's not a husband's prerogative to enforce this command because submission ultimately is a wife's voluntary act of worship and obedience *to the Lord*.
- A wife's loving and informed submission to her own husband is for the purpose of creating a "one flesh" union that points beyond the marriage to the mystery of Christ and His church.
- A husband's loving leadership—as described in Scripture— challenges both of the predominant masculine sins of domination and passivity. (More on this in the next chapter.)

That's the big picture of God's purposes in marriage. No doubt, you have a bunch of questions about what this looks like in daily living. We'll touch on some of those topics in the next chapter. I have gleaned a lot from my married friends, and I am eager to share their wisdom with you.

"FOLLOW THIS MAN"

HERE'S A STORY TO ENCOURAGE EVERY woman who struggles with the idea of following and supporting an imperfect man. Maybe you think your husband doesn't deserve your commitment in marriage. Maybe you think his flaws or sins are much worse than yours, so he has to earn your respect. Or maybe you are married to a man who is spiritually dead and it's hard to have faith that one day he will actually believe the gospel. My friends Bill and Stephanie Kettering have not only learned the value of roles in a godly marriage, they have also learned a lot about forgiveness. I hope their story will help you to have faith for what God can do in your own relationship as you trust and obey Him.

Stephanie called her husband to say good night—a routine whenever she spent a night away from him. Bill had not come along on this visit to her parents this time, claiming a heavy work schedule and the demands of graduate school.

During their conversation, he seemed distracted and a bit cool to her. Uncertain about Bill's demeanor, Stephanie decided to wrap up the conversation. "Well, okay, good night. I love you."

"Me, too," he responded.

Lying in her childhood bed that night, Stephanie replayed the conversation over and over in her head. *Me too.* It was like an alarm bell. Why didn't he say the real words, like he always did? Restless, she reached for the phone once again. The glowing alarm clock said it was after 2:00 a.m.

No answer. She redialed. Still no answer.

Dread descended upon her suspicions. Stephanie woke up her sister, asking her to watch her two daughters. She was going to make the long drive back to her home to check on her husband.

On the highway, her emotions spilled over. Stephanie wondered what she would find when she arrived. Was Bill deathly ill and unable to answer the phone? Was he injured and at the hospital? Or . . . was he spending the night with someone else?

Fragments of their conversations and interactions over the past year barged into her consciousness. How distant Bill had seemed during their daughter's sixth birthday party. How much time he was putting in at the office. The approving way he spoke of his colleagues. The way he told Stephanie about how attractive one colleague was in her new red dress. How much emotional support he gave this woman following the breakup of her dating relationship. How critical he was of Stephanie when he was at home.

Reflexively, she began praying. *God, help me. Help my marriage. Give me a sign about what to do.*

Stephanie could only think of one way to know that God was answering her prayer. She turned on the radio, telling herself that whatever song she heard next would be her sign. After a moment of fearful silence, she heard the simple melody of a song sung at her wedding.

> A man shall leave his mother and a woman leave her home.
> And they shall travel on to where the two shall be as one.
> As it was in the beginning, is now, and 'til the end,
> Woman draws her life from man and gives it back again.
> And there is love, there is love.[15]

Stephanie stared in sharp surprise at the radio. *God's really listening*, she thought. Pulling onto her street, she could see that Bill's car was not in the driveway. She got out of her car in the predawn chill, walked to the door of her empty house, and up the stairs to her bedroom.

Seeing the empty bed, she broke into tears once again. Questions swirled all around her. *Who is my husband? Do I even know him anymore? Does he live a separate life? How could he do this? Does he even love me anymore? What about the children? What is going to happen to us?*

Stephanie sat up all night, unable to sleep. The next morning, she called Bill at his office and asked to come see him. He met her in the parking garage and got into the car. She took his hand, placed it over her heart, looked him in the eyes, and asked the dreaded question.

"Where were you last night?"

Suddenly aware of how much the truth was going to hurt Stephanie, Bill lied. "I was home."

"No, you weren't," Stephanie responded quietly. "I went home and you weren't there."

Stunned, Bill felt a wave of mixed emotions crash over him—relief because the truth was out, sorrow for hurting his wife, and regret and shame for his actions. He couldn't say anything.

Stephanie burst into tears. After a tense moment, she looked away and asked a series of poignant questions: "Why don't you love me? Do you love her? Do you want a divorce?"

"I do love you, and no, I don't want a divorce—I really don't," he finally responded.

"Then why did you do it?"

"I don't know . . . ," he answered. "I'm really sorry."

In the ensuing months, Stephanie and Bill continued to talk and rebuild their relationship. Stephanie wanted to tear down the wall of mistrust between them, and she felt helpless to do anything about it. At the same time, Bill was processing his shame.

Shortly after his affair was uncovered, Bill switched jobs. His new boss was an overt Christian, not reticent about emphasizing the fear of God. He was also big and intimidating. Bill was tempted to shy away from his boss, but God used him to introduce Bill to the idea that his marriage needed something more than what he or Stephanie had to give.

One day, Bill walked into the kitchen and announced the diagnosis: "You know what's missing in our marriage? Christ is missing."

Stephanie immediately agreed. Then she told him about two families she had gotten to know on their street who went to the same church and seemed to *really* like it. So that was the church they went to visit the following Sunday.

Though it was his idea to go, when Sunday rolled around Bill had mixed emotions. Foremost on his mind was how to undo what he had done and be forgiven. He felt stained standing in a church where everyone seemed so happy and was singing with such enthusiasm. At the end of the meeting, the pastor presented the gospel, outlined how people could be forgiven of their sins, and then asked those who wanted to accept Christ's offer of free grace to raise their hands.

Bill put up his hand. So did Stephanie.

Then the pastor asked those who raised their hands to come forward for prayer. Holding hands, Bill and Stephanie walked toward the front. One of the other pastors stepped forward and stopped them. He looked at Bill, then at Stephanie, and then back at Bill.

"I watched you come down here, and I want you to know that God has a plan for you," he said to Bill. Then turning to Stephanie, he gently added, "Follow this man."

Seventeen years later, the Ketterings are sitting in their family room, re-counting how much has changed since that day. Bill is sitting on the floor, next to Stephanie, who is on the couch. As they recount the painful details, Bill reaches out for his wife, maintaining a reassuring contact.

"What I remember most from that day in church was that I was sud-denly aware that my focus all this time had been on my husband's sin," Stephanie recalls. "I was sure that Bill would raise his hand. But at that exact moment, I saw my own sins and realized I needed a Savior too. Until then, I had lived mostly aware of how I had been wronged."

Reflecting back on what the pastor said to them the day they became Christians, Bill praises his wife.

"She wouldn't have had a category to put what 'following' meant at that time, at least in terms of biblical teaching," he says. "But she knew that it was from the Lord. And so she did it. She really fought to figure out what it looks like to forgive and follow me."

Pausing for a moment, Bill fights to maintain his composure. The tears cascade down his cheeks anyway.

"I think one of the clearest examples of her desire to follow me was that—other than her sister and brother-in-law—she never told anyone what I did," he says in a choked voice. "She left it to me to tell others. Her reason was so that she would not dishonor me. Incredible, isn't it?"

After their initial visit, the Ketterings were quick to join the church and start attending a small group that met in their neighborhood. They were open about having difficulties in their marriage, but they didn't share the particulars right away. As a result, Stephanie would turn to Bill for help when she was struggling with memories of his infidelity.

"Throughout that difficult first year, Bill was there for me," Stephanie re-calls. "He helped me with the healing process. There were times when I didn't want to get out of bed, but I knew I had to because of my daughters. I al-ways knew bitterness was stirring again when in my mind I would play out these scenarios of him with this other woman. At those moments, I would pray very simple prayers, saying things like, 'Help me, Lord. Don't let me think that way.' Then I'd call Bill and tell him that I was having bad thoughts about him. And he would say, 'I am sorry, I don't know how to change that but I want you to know I do love you.' Then after we became Christians, I would say to him, 'Please tell me that you will never do this again.' I remember he said, 'I'd like to promise that, but I can't *guarantee* it because I'm a sinner. But I can promise that God is faithful and *He* is able to keep our marriage strong.'"

As a new Christian, her struggles forced Stephanie to develop a rubber-meets-the-road understanding of forgiveness. One day she read a verse where Jesus was instructing His disciples about forgiveness. Mark 11:25 (NIV) reads: "And when you stand praying, if you hold anything against anyone, forgive him, so that your Father in heaven may forgive you your sins."

"I saw there was a footnote for this verse and I followed it down to see that some manuscripts contained an additional verse that says, 'But if you do not forgive, neither will your Father who is in heaven forgive your sins,'" she recalls. "It was a clear command to forgive. But it was a command based upon how much forgiveness I had received from God. The mercy I had received for my sins was the reason I could forgive Bill for his."

Even with that understanding and new appreciation for her own forgiveness, Stephanie found that bitterness was an occasional temptation. So she worried that she was not fulfilling the related command in Matthew 18:21–22 to forgive seventy times seven. But even that concern had an unintended benefit—it highlighted her ongoing need for a Savior.

"I found I easily drifted into relying on my own performance for assurance," she says. "I finally learned it was only through the gospel that I could reconcile my experience with the biblical commands to love and honor my husband. When I clearly understood Christ suffered on that cross in lots of pain so that *I* could be forgiven, that became my motivation. That's how I could love my husband—Christ did it for me and I wanted to live my life to please Him."

Fairly soon after the Ketterings became Christians, one of the women in their small group gave them two bags full of sermons on tape. Bill began listening to these tapes on his commute, plowing through dozens each month.

"He would come home and tell me all about what he was learning," Stephanie recalls. "One day, he walked in the house and said, 'Do you know what I learned today? I'm charged with being the head. I'm responsible to lead our family.' When he said that to me, I felt a weight come off my shoulders. I always felt like I was supposed to be doing this. But I asked him, 'Well, who is the head of you?' He replied, 'Christ is my head.'"

Bill smiles at his wife as she recounts this conversation, and then adds, "She never made me feel awkward because she had assumed this posture of wanting to please God, of wanting to do what God had called her to do in terms of loving me. She never said, 'You don't deserve to lead this family.'"

Before they became Christians, they had a fairly typical marriage. Bill worked full-time and took graduate courses part-time so that he could improve his career opportunities. Stephanie primarily stayed home with their daughters, but she also worked weekends in a retail job. Even though they were married, they often led parallel but separate lives.

"Back then, I never thought Stephanie needed me. Things functioned fine without me," Bill states. "Afterward, I knew I was supposed to be involved and not leave her to handle everything on her own. It wasn't that she wasn't capable—she certainly was—but now we understood that I needed to shoulder the responsibilities that I'm called to do."

As they learned about the biblical design for marriage, there was a subtle but deep change in their lives. They had always functioned well together in terms of getting tasks done, but now they enjoy the added benefit of the peace that comes from clarity.

"When it's very clear who is responsible for what—when we know our parts of the partnership—it's more peaceful," Bill says. "We didn't have defined roles before. We were just doing things together. Now we know what it's supposed to look like," he says. "And we're working together to make it so."

Certainly when she came home that difficult night to find her husband gone, Stephanie never could have imagined they would be so happy now. Nor would she have imagined that God could use them to help other couples. The Ketterings are now part of their church's biblical counseling team, through which they have helped hundreds of couples with their own marital conflicts.

Sitting in her family room, with her adult daughters coming and going, Stephanie holds her husband's hand and offers her hard-won perspective.

"Most people would think divorce would be the first option in a situation like this. But God is most glorified when you don't do that, but instead trust that He will be faithful to His Word to give you the wisdom, forgiveness, and grace for change that you need."

Four

ROLE
Call

*H*ave you ever noticed how romantic comedies usually end with the wedding—and never portray the reality shock that follows? Our natural tendency is to want to conclude when all eyes are on us—the center of attention. Though the Bible is big on weddings, it supplies us with much-needed information on how marriage is supposed to work after the honeymoon.

In this chapter, it's time to get a little more practical. Marriage is the primary interaction, but in all of our relationships, there are echoes of these corresponding roles for men and women. In this chapter, we start with what I've learned (the hard way) and then move on to the real experts! Along the way, we'll look at how second-wave feminist theories about gender are already falling apart, why being a "helpmate" reflects how God describes Himself, and how a wife's submission should even include correction.

THE FIRST TIME I EVER went white-water rafting, I learned an important lesson . . . but not about rafting . . . or even about surviving the launch into roiling rapids. What I learned was the importance of being a good follower.

My boyfriend at the time was really into cycling and white-water boating, primarily kayaking. The cycling was fine with me; we had met on a bike trip. But I always thought of white-water boating as his thing, not mine. So when Greg suggested we take a white-water rafting trip together, I refused to go. He would have none of my refusal, though, and he insisted that we would have fun. Despite my whining, complaining, and fearful resistance, somehow I ended up wearing a life jacket and pouting on a raft on a hot summer day, my bad attitude sucking the fun out of the whole event.

As we started down the river, Greg turned to me and said firmly: "Look, you could do this if you would just stop complaining and listen to me. I know what I'm doing here. I know your capabilities. Just listen to what I tell you, do it, and you'll be fine. You're the one making this difficult."

On paper that sounds harsh, but it was really said in the manner of a personal trainer motivating a balky participant. Greg already had taught me how to push myself on long bike rides and up steep hills. He was right—he knew my capabilities better than I did. So when I stopped resisting him, we both had fun on the river. In fact, I *loved* rafting!

That day, Greg gave me two gifts: a love of white-water rafting and an insight into the importance of both leadership and followership. Both roles are needed for any union of human beings. Leaders have to have people following them or they aren't leading anyone. An insightful, cooperative follower is as necessary to the team as a good leader.

White-water rafting provides the perfect illustration of this point. A rafting guide is the leader of several other paddlers in the boat. Some paddlers may be novices; others may be quite seasoned. But on the river, only one person can make decisions in fast-moving water. Everyone else has to listen to the guide and paddle in unison—or else the team goes for an unwanted swim in the rough water. Because he is charged with navigating the rapids, the guide yells, "All forward! Pull hard!" But if he's the only one paddling, the maneuver won't be successful. As the raft approaches the rapids, it's important that the paddlers listen carefully to the guide and do what he says—promptly and thoroughly. Coordinated teamwork prevents disaster.

Though neither of us were Christians at the time, Greg provided a candid assessment of my character, as well as an illustration that helped me understand God's harmonious design for marriage when I became a Christian less than a year later. This is the same principle found in Scripture about marriage. God has assigned the husband the role of the guide. The husband is accountable for guiding the raft according to the instructions he has received from the Bible. Likewise, God has assigned to the wife the role of the fellow-paddler. She takes her paddling cues from her husband, and together they navigate the turbulence of life. If he doesn't lead well, the boat could go in circles. If she doesn't follow well, the boat could capsize.

As a new believer, I initially balked at the idea of different roles in marriage; however, the lessons learned during my rafting trip came to mind during my theological learning curve. You see, even as an unmarried woman, I had to decide if I was going to believe and trust God's Word about these roles—and not just for my own benefit. Every time I witnessed a Christian marriage, my presence promised I would support God's design for marriage. Every time my married friends spoke to me about their trials and temptations, I had the choice to influence them with the Bible's perspective or with the latest self-help theories. Therefore, I needed to dig in and make sure I understood what God was saying in His Word. *We do not need the authority of personal experience to counsel one another because the Bible is sufficient for this task.* But we do need to *know* the Word.

Role Reversal

It's discomforting to think that at age thirty I had to learn that fundamental differences exist between men and women. But I grew up sandblasted with the feminist dogma that gender differences are culturally created—that apart from the obvious structural differences, we are inherently the same. Medical research has dismantled that theory in recent years as we've discovered significant biological differences between men and women, especially in the area of brain anatomy and function. As one article about brain science stated, the differences between the sexes are more complex than originally suspected:

In the last decade, studies of perception, cognition, memory and neural function have found apparent gender differences that often buck conventional prejudices.

Women's brains, for instance, seem to be faster and more efficient than men's.

All in all, men appear to have more gray matter, made up of active neurons, and women more of the white matter responsible for communication between different areas of the brain.

Overall, women's brains seem to be more complexly corrugated, suggesting that more complicated neural structures lie within, researchers at UCLA found in August.

Men and women appear to use different parts of the brain to encode memories, sense emotions, recognize faces, solve certain problems and make decisions. Indeed, when men and women of similar intelligence and aptitude perform equally well, their brains appear to go about it differently, as if nature had separate blueprints, researchers at UC Irvine reported this year.[1]

Our different brain structures indicate that men and women process stimuli, thoughts, emotions, and memories differently from one another. Essentially, we are *designed* to function differently. However, researchers stress there is no difference between men and women in IQ or intelligence. Our brains confirm what Scripture tells us: men and women are equal in essence but are created to function differently.

Though science confirms this essential difference, the message has not yet caught up with our general culture. Feminist theories from the 1970s still have considerable sway in our social relationships today, especially romantic relationships:

In *The Female Eunuch*, [feminist author Germaine] Greer theorized that women's bodily and psychological differences were induced characteristics imposed upon women to keep them subservient. She maintained, for instance, that woman's skeletal structure was greatly influenced by the role women were forced to occupy in society. . . . Greer conceded that some genital differences were obvious and undeniable, but argued that these differences had been exaggerated by the cultural roles women had been forced to occupy. According to Greer, men had shaped women into who they were. She argued that patriarchy had distorted both women's natural psychological and biological composition.

Greer proposed that all societal mores, structures, and institutions that falsely magnified the biological differences needed to be challenged and disassembled. She encouraged women to question and change the way they viewed male-female roles, the marital relationship, and even their own bodies.[2]

What we are reaping from this is disappointed confusion. In our social relationships, we are still acting upon old feminist theories, both in dating and in marriage. And the irony of it is that even secular sources are spotting the contradictions. A prime example comes from two of the scriptwriters of *Sex and the City* (not a show I would recommend) who published a self-help book for single women, *He's Just Not That into You: The No-Excuses Truth to Understanding Guys*. The creators of the sexually aggressive but relationally challenged Carrie Bradshaw character on *Sex and the City* felt it was necessary to explain to her fans why their own similar relationships weren't working. It became a *New York Times* number 1 bestseller and an Oprah book recommendation because the married coauthor, Greg Behrendt, explained one immutable truth to women:

> Men, for the most part, like to pursue women. We like not knowing if we can catch you. We feel rewarded when we do. Especially when the chase is a long one. We know there was a sexual revolution. (We loved it.) We know women are capable of running governments, heading multinational corporations, and raising loving children—sometimes all at the same time. That, however, doesn't make *men* different.[3]

Now I'm not recommending this book, but doesn't it stagger the imagination that women today need to understand that there is a profound difference between men and women? Or that a blunt book like *He's Just Not That into You* becomes a sales success by explaining the difference between a cad and a catch to adult women? In fact, this book even offers a defense for women who want to be married:

Just remember this. Every man you have ever dated who has said he doesn't want to get married or doesn't believe in marriage, or has "issues" with marriage, will, rest assured, someday be married. It just will never be with you. Because he's not really saying he doesn't want to get married. He's saying he doesn't want to get married to you. There is nothing wrong with wanting to get married. You shouldn't feel ashamed, needy, or "unliberated" for wanting that. So make sure from the start that you pick a guy who shares your views for the future, and if not, move on as quickly as you can. Big plans require big action.[4]

This kind of relational confusion moves into marriage . . . if indeed the modern couple is not derailed by living together. A 2007 Pew Research Center study reported that nearly half (47 percent) of adults in their thirties and forties have spent a portion of their lives in a cohabiting relationship.[5] But the common idea that cohabitation will determine whether a marriage will succeed is a faulty one, according to researcher Jennifer Roback Morse:

> The Census reports a 72 percent increase in the number of cohabiting couples since 1990. Unfortunately, research shows that cohabitation is correlated with greater likelihood of unhappiness, and domestic violence in the relationship. Cohabiting couples report lower levels of satisfaction in the relationship than married couples. Women are more likely to be abused by a cohabiting boyfriend than a husband. Children are more likely to abused by their mothers' boyfriends than by her husband, even if the boyfriend is their biological father. If a cohabiting couple ultimately marries, they tend to report lower levels of marital satisfaction and a higher propensity to divorce.
>
> Recent reports and commentaries on cohabitation tend to downplay these difficulties. I suspect this is because people do not know how to make sense of the research findings. Many people imagine that living together before marriage resembles taking a car for a test drive. The "trial period" gives people a chance to discover whether they are compatible. This analogy seems so compelling that people are unable to interpret the mountains of data to the contrary.[6]

Cohabitation by its definition is anticommitment. A prolonged "maybe" is not a commitment. It's sad that this is seen as a better option to God's gift of marriage. What Scripture portrays is a passionate, secure love between husband and wife, where commitment provides the freedom to celebrate one another and not hedge bets:

> *You have stolen my heart, my sister, my bride; you have stolen my heart with one glance of your eyes, with one jewel of your necklace. How delightful is your love, my sister, my bride! How much more pleasing is your love than wine, and the fragrance of your perfume than any spice!*
> (Song of Songs 4:9–10 NIV)

A Helper Fit for Him

I don't think anyone would despise that wonderful picture of marriage. But when the beloved becomes the wife, women can struggle to see marriage as an attractive concept. Why? Because in the Bible a wife is described as a complement to her husband, a help to her mate. To be others-focused in our self-centered culture is unusual.

When I think back upon my life prior to my conversion, I cannot recall a single instance of anyone using the word "helpmate" to describe a wife. But the idea was embedded in our culture. In fact, the helpmate concept was satirized in *Ms.* magazine's inaugural edition with the classic article, "Why I Want a Wife," in which the writer satirized the role of the wife:

> Not too long ago a male friend of mine appeared on the scene fresh from a recent divorce. He had one child, who is, of course, with his ex-wife. He is looking for another wife. As I thought about him while I was ironing one evening, it suddenly occurred to me that I, too, would like to have a wife. Why do I want a wife?
>
> I would like to go back to school so that I can become economically independent, support myself, and if need be, support those dependent upon me. I want a wife who will work and send me to school. . . . I want a wife who will take care of my physical needs. I want a wife who will keep my house clean. A wife who will pick up after my children, a wife who will pick up after me. I want a wife who will keep

my clothes clean, ironed, mended, replaced when need be, and who will see to it that my personal things are kept in their proper place so that I can find what I need the minute I need it. I want a wife who cooks the meals, a wife who is a good cook. I want a wife who will plan the menus, do the necessary grocery shopping, prepare the meals, serve them pleasantly, and then do the cleaning up while I do my studying. I want a wife who will care for me when I am sick and sympathize with my pain and loss of time from school. I want a wife to go along when our family takes a vacation so that someone can continue to care for me . . . when I need a rest and change of scene. I want a wife who will not bother me with rambling complaints about a wife's duties.[7]

When stated like this, who wouldn't want to have such a personal assistant?! But please note that this author's musings about a wife's duties began as she was considering a man who was not living out the biblical commands for a husband and father. It's so easy for the conversation to drift when God is not part of the picture. That's why it's important that we not overlay cultural assumptions on biblical concepts.

When the Bible uses the word *helper*, there is a divine context for it. When the word is first introduced in Genesis 2:18—"It is not good that the man should be alone; I will make him a helper fit for him"— it is the same Hebrew word (*'ezer*) that is used most often to refer to God throughout the Old Testament. If God, who is obviously and infinitely superior to us, unblushingly refers to Himself as our helper, we should be proud to use the same term. As Wayne Grudem notes, the context of this verse describes both the helper idea *and* the inherent equality between men and women:

> The Hebrew text can be translated literally, "I will make for him (Hebrew *le-*) a helper fit for him." The apostle Paul understands this accurately, because in 1 Corinthians 11 he writes, "Neither was man created for woman, but woman for man" (1 Corinthians 11:9). Eve's role, and the purpose that God had in mind when He created her, was that she should be "for him . . . a helper." . . . Yet in the same sentence God emphasizes that the woman is not to help the man as one who is

inferior to him. Rather, she is to be a helper "fit for him" and here the Hebrew word *kenegdô* means a help "corresponding to him," that is "equal and adequate to himself." So Eve was created as a helper, but as a helper who was Adam's equal, and one who differed from him, but who differed from him in ways that would exactly complement who Adam was.[8]

As we saw in the last chapter, this is the point that feminists miss. They equate roles with inherent worth, a leap the Bible never makes. If you don't have Genesis 1 to establish the equality of men and women in creation, and if you don't have Genesis 2 to provide the "one flesh" portrait of marriage and the roles needed to make this work, then you just have all the ingredients for a simmering brew of misunderstanding and resentment. And, as Morse notes, that simmering brew affects both parties:

The feminist movement introduced an unbelievable amount of tension into the relationships between men and women. Feminism gave us women permission to nag and criticize our husbands, which most women can do just fine without any special permission. The legacy of the feminist movement has been to turn the home, which should be the place of cooperation, into a sphere of competition between men and women. And ironically, feminism, which was supposed to be about getting beyond stereotypes, supported the most negative of stereotypes about men.

I have my own pet theory about the stereotype of men dragging their feet about getting married. The socio-biologists claim that men want to invest their seed in as many women as possible, and therefore do not want marriage. I think this is only a dim shadow of the whole truth. The whole truth must include this great fact about men: they are capable of heroic loyalty. When men finally do marry, they are capable of committing themselves to the care of their wives and children. Many men spend a lifetime working at jobs they don't like very much, for the love of their families. When men marry, they take it very seriously. *It is women who initiate most divorces.* It is divorced men who commit suicide at twice the rate as married men, while divorce has little impact on the suicide propensities of women[9] (emphasis added).

A Corresponding Challenge

I think Morse's description above can actually be broadened to the relationship between men and women in general—the legacy of the feminist movement has been to turn the potential of complementary cooperation between men and women into a spirit of competition. But there's hope for restoring unity. I really like the description John Ensor provides in *Doing Things Right in Matters of the Heart*:

> In matters of the heart, it is right that men should lead and women welcome and guide that leadership. She is his helpmate (Genesis 2:18). Her goal is to give her man all the help he needs to lead well. His goal is to humbly accept the responsibility to lead and not to run from it or wield it like a club.
>
> The guidance that she provides him comes mainly in two forms: in helping him think clearly and in encouraging him to act confidently. What comes from this is a shared victory. If it proves a mistake, it is borne together. Either way, what is fostered is true unity of spirit, which is the heart of the matter, where the two become one. We have to work at it, but if we do, true unity is fostered and preserved in the complementary exchange of male leadership and female guidance.[10]

Now, I will concede that many men fall short of the humble, sacrificially loving leadership role. Many women fall short of the humble, encouraging support role too. Just because sin mars a concept does not mean that it is beyond gospel redemption. We will return to that idea in a few pages, but I want to stop here and acknowledge something I hope is obvious: I am not writing this book for men. If you're curious how this "complementary exchange" should be taught to men, there are numerous books already in existence for men by men on being a godly husband. The ones that seem to be most appreciated by the men I know are *The Exemplary Husband* by Stuart Scott; *Sex, Romance, and the Glory of God: What Every Christian Husband Needs to Know* by C. J. Mahaney; and *The Complete Husband* by Lou Priolo—not to mention the challenging material for husbands found in *When Sinners Say "I Do"* by Dave Harvey, *Love That Lasts* by

Gary and Betsy Ricucci, and *Sacred Marriage* by Gary Thomas. In fact, Gary Thomas writes this helpful perspective about balancing biblical roles:

> The wife's submission to her husband gets placed in the context of a marriage in which a husband is called to be like Christ—laying down his life on her behalf, putting her first, serving her, caring for her, always loving her in the same sacrificial, lay-down-your-life manner in which Christ loves the church (verse 25).
>
> Paul describes an idealistic view of a simultaneous commitment to each other's welfare. I don't mean to use "idealistic" in a negative way—certainly every marriage should strive for it. But I also think Paul would be the first to object if he heard women being urged to submit, while condescending and dictatorial husbands heard no corresponding challenge to love in the manner of Christ. The church must not teach the submission of wives *apart from* the sacrificial love and servanthood required of husbands. This doesn't mean a husband's lack of sacrificial love *cancels* a wife's call to submission, but it does make applying this principle a little trickier.[11]

I have seen that corresponding challenge to men—I can attest that it exists. Not only have I heard it from the pulpit, I have seen it exercised in private. In fact, as I was working on this chapter, I happened to attend a meeting with two pastors to discuss a project I was developing. The conversation was sidetracked at one point when the older pastor began to gently challenge the younger one about his priorities. The older pastor urged the younger one not to sacrifice his family for the pressures of the ministry. He reminded him that kingdom work begins in the family and that he was called to care for his wife and not leave her unduly burdened. I've also seen men hold each other accountable for planning weekly date nights with their wives and for arranging child care, and I've heard men challenge other men about the pursuit of selfish hobbies or excessive work hours. I know men who have turned down prestigious job opportunities because the relocation or work commitment would impair the spiritual health of the family.

In short, when men are taught that they will be held accountable

for the spiritual vitality and fruitfulness of their families, they understand that leadership is meant to direct their families *toward Christ*.
Leadership is not about filling a position for one's own glory but for
serving God's gospel purposes. Without this spiritual reference point,
our culture interprets leadership as a self-glorifying position—and
then objects to women being called to support it. Those who know
Christ must not make the same faulty assumption.

Submission and Sin

Going back to the point Gary Thomas raised in the previous
quote, maybe you're a wife trying to apply the helpmate principle in
a difficult marriage and you're wondering how to do it. As I came to
learn, submission has more to do with our *attitude* toward this concept than any flawless execution of it. As John Piper and Wayne Grudem say, it really comes down to where our hearts incline:

> Submission refers to a wife's divine calling to honor and affirm her
> husband's leadership and help carry it through according to her gifts.
> It is not an absolute surrender of her will. Rather, we speak of her *dis-
> position to yield* to her husband's guidance and her *inclination* to follow
> his leadership. Christ is her absolute authority, not the husband. She
> submits "out of reverence for Christ" (Ephesians 5:21). The supreme
> authority of Christ qualifies the authority of her husband. She should
> never follow her husband into sin. Nevertheless, even when she may
> have to stand with Christ against the sinful will of her husband (e.g.,
> 1 Peter 3:1, where she does not yield to her husband's unbelief), she
> can still have a *spirit* of submission—a *disposition* to yield. She can show
> by her attitude and behavior that she does not like resisting his will and
> that she longs for him to forsake sin and lead in righteousness so that
> her disposition to honor him as head can again produce harmony.[12]

She should never follow her husband into sin. A true helpmate is
not a blind follower, but rather she is a faithful friend and wise sister
in Christ who understands the seriousness of sin. As John Piper says:
"Wives are not only submissive wives. They are also loving sisters.
There is a unique way for a submissive wife to be a caring sister to-

ward her imperfect brother-husband. She will, from time to time, follow Galatians 6:1 in his case: 'If anyone is caught in any transgression, you who are spiritual should restore him in a spirit of gentleness.' She will do that for him."[13]

A wife's role means that she is uniquely graced to provide her husband with helpful counsel and insightful correction. As author Carolyn Mahaney says, God will use a wife's different life experiences, strengths, gifts, and viewpoints to complement her husband and bolster his leadership role:

> Now this should give us faith for how God can use us to serve our husbands. God will give us specific wisdom and counsel for them. We will have unique insight that can serve them in their relationship with God and in their relationship with others. We possess discernment that will help them effectively lead our family. And we have a responsibility to exercise these gifts of wisdom and discernment that God has given us for our husband's good, both in his personal life and in his leadership role. Now most of the time, this will involve communicating our support and encouragement, or simply sharing our perspective on a matter or giving him counsel and advice, but on occasion, it will include bringing him correction, as well.[14]

In fact, Carolyn's husband, C. J. Mahaney, says that as a pastor he has seen a common misunderstanding of submission and honor, where the wife is unduly worried about her husband's opinion or reaction if she were to correct him. "For any marriage, correction of the husband by the wife would be one category on my short list of most important," he says. "If I observed a wife who was reluctant to correct her husband I would be concerned with that marriage. Obviously, I'm not arguing for a contentious marriage, but correction, humbly communicated, must be part of every marriage. . . . I would argue that correction is not just part of marriage but an aspect of what it means to be fellow heirs of the grace of life. Carolyn's encouragement has been of immeasurable benefit to me, but equally so or more, on balance, has been her correction. She has protected me when sin was deceiving me."[15]

Speaking of sin, the biblical mandate for wives to submit to their husbands *never* means wives are to submit to physical abuse. Domestic assault is not only a crime, it is a breach of God's law. In such cases, an abused wife should remove herself from the home, seek safe shelter, and involve both legal authorities and her church elders for her protection.

Quitting the Role

A few pages back, you may have noticed that I quoted researcher Jennifer Roback Morse saying that women initiate most divorces. Did that statement catch your eye? It did catch mine when I first read it, for that trend certainly has been my observation. It, too, is a legacy of feminism.

One of the triumphs claimed by second-wave feminists was the sweeping change in the marriage contract. During the 1970s and 1980s, all fifty states adopted "no-fault" divorce laws, enabling one spouse to unilaterally file for divorce without claiming that the other spouse had broken the marriage contract through adultery, abuse, or felony crime. Some critics argue this is *the* most profound effect of feminism upon our culture:

> This change in our divorce laws has affected the social, economic, cultural, and legal fabric of our society more than anything else that has happened in the last two decades. One can avoid participating in or succumbing to other changes, but the changed laws and attitudes about divorce affect us all. No one can force you to have an abortion or to read pornography. If you can't pray in school, you can still pray at home, in church, and in your heart. You can escape what you deem to be intolerable situations by changing your job or your school.
>
> But divorce—the dissolution of a solemn mutual contract in which you pledge your life, your honor, your name, your commitment, and your future—can be thrust upon you without your consent. It takes two to marry, but now one spouse can terminate the marriage without the consent of the other. The very existence of this sword of Damocles hanging over every husband and wife validates the attitude that marriage is temporary and based on self-satisfaction, rather than on commitment and responsibility.

The radical feminist movement peddled easy, no-fault divorce as liberation for women when, in fact, it was chiefly liberation for men. The feminists didn't discover their mistake until Lenore Weitzman published her landmark 1985 book, *The Divorce Revolution*, which proved that easy divorce usually means economic devastation for women.

It is also time for someone to speak up and say out loud that a large part of the human cost of divorce is paid by the children.[16]

Since no-fault divorce has been peddled to women as a path to maximum personal happiness and fulfillment, that led one group of researchers to follow a representative group of couples over five years to find out if divorce was measurably connected to a rise in happiness. They tracked spouses who rated their marriages as "unhappy" in the initial interview and then reinterviewed them five years later. Over those five years, some had divorced, some had separated, and some remained married. The researchers concluded that: "Unhappily married adults who divorced or separated were no happier, on average, than unhappily married adults who stayed married. Even unhappy spouses who had divorced and remarried were no happier, on average, than unhappy spouses who stayed married."[17]

Contrary to an increase in personal fulfillment, there are pages and pages of data about the negative effects of divorce. If you are divorced and reading this, your experience may or may not line up with the data—and by broaching this topic, I certainly don't want to be insensitive to anyone's personal pain. But I believe that the Titus 2 mandate for older women to teach younger women how to love their husbands must include, in this day and age, specific biblical instruction on divorce—*especially* when women are initiating more divorces than men.

Let's examine the debate over divorce that Jesus engaged in, as recorded in the gospel of Matthew:

And Pharisees came up to him and tested him by asking, "Is it lawful to divorce one's wife for any cause?" He answered, "Have you not read that he who created them from the beginning made them male and female, and said, 'Therefore a man shall leave his father and his mother and hold fast to his wife, and the two shall become one flesh'? So they are no longer two but one flesh. What therefore God has joined together, let not man

*separate." They said to him, "Why then did Moses command one to give a
certificate of divorce and to send her away?" He said to them, "Because of
your hardness of heart Moses allowed you to divorce your wives, but from
the beginning it was not so. And I say to you: whoever divorces his wife,
except for sexual immorality, and marries another, commits adultery."*
(Matthew 19:3–9)

The answer Jesus gave to the Pharisees transcended the squabbles
that existed then between different rabbinic schools about the law-
fulness of divorce. By pointing back to the original design of marriage
in God's plan, Jesus surprised even His own disciples at the high standard He set before them. Their response in the very next sentence
was rueful: "If such is the case of a man with his wife, it is better not
to marry." But Jesus responds to them with assurance that only a few
people are called to lifelong celibacy. As Andreas Köstenberger notes,
this was good news for women:

> Not only does he stress the permanence of marriage as a divine rather
> than merely human institution, he contends that divorce is fundamen-
> tally at odds with God's purpose in creation. What is more, Jesus' appli-
> cation of the same standard regarding divorce and remarriage to both
> men and women (see especially Mark 10:11) is nothing less than revo-
> lutionary. Despite regulations in the Mosaic law that stipulated equal
> treatment of men and women with regard to divorce (Lev. 20:10-12),
> in Old Testament times a double standard prevailed according to which
> women were required to be faithful to their husbands (or punishment
> ensued) while the standards for men were considerably more lenient. In
> Jesus' teaching, however, conjugal rights were set on an equal footing.
> In fact, Jesus taught that lust for other women in a man's heart already
> constituted adultery (Matt. 5:28), which implies that extramarital af-
> fairs are equally wrong for men and women.[18]

There's an oft-repeated Christian truism that says, "What God
commands, He enables." God is not having a huge belly laugh over
the fact that He set fallen, sinful creatures in the binding covenant of
marriage and then commanded them to remain locked in mortal combat. Not at all! God possesses an *infinite* supply of grace to help us

change and grow. The majority of divorces today are simply attributed to "irreconcilable differences"—don't you think there is grace for these relationships?

I don't have the room in this book to address the practical discipleship issues in these areas of marriage (and I defer to those who have experienced God's grace in marriage personally), but I do want to conclude this chapter with an encouraging insight to wives from Gary Thomas:

> Though every wife has married a man with a unique background and gifts and personality, every wife has one thing in common: her husband is an imperfect man. No woman has a spouse who never gives her reason for legitimate complaint. . . . This presents you with a spiritual challenge. You will have to fight the natural human tendency to obsess over your husband's weaknesses. When I urge you to affirm your husband's strengths, I'm not minimizing his many weaknesses. I'm just encouraging you to make the daily spiritual choice of focusing on qualities for which you feel thankful. The time will come when you can address the weaknesses—*after* you've established a firm foundation of love and encouragement. For now, you must make a conscious choice to give thanks for his strengths.
>
> I have found Philippians 4:8 as relevant for marriage as it is for life: "Whatever is true, whatever is noble, whatever is right, whatever is pure, whatever is lovely, whatever is admirable—if anything is excellent or praiseworthy—think about these things."
>
> Obsessing over your husband's weaknesses won't make them go away. You may have done that for years—and if so, what has it gotten you, besides more of the same? Leslie Vernick warns, "Regularly thinking negatively about your husband *increases* your dissatisfaction with him and your marriage." Affirming your husband's strengths, however, will likely reinforce and build up those areas you cherish and motivate him to pursue excellence of character in others.
>
> Guys rise to praise. When someone compliments us, we want to keep that person's positive opinion intact. We love how it feels when our wives respect us; we get a rush like nothing else when we hear her praise or see that look of awe in her eyes—and we will all but travel the ends of the earth to keep it coming.[19]

At the beginning of this chapter, I used the analogy of a fellow-paddler in a white-water raft for a wife's role. It takes a lot of strength to paddle in turbulent water and stay in the boat. In marriage, it takes a lot of strength of character to be a helpmate as the Bible describes it and not bail on the marriage. But you're not doing it alone or in your own strength. Never forget that the encouragement, correction, submission, honor, respect, and appreciation that you give your husband each day are lavishly supplied by the One who is also *your* helper!

SPEAK TRUTH TO HIM

THERE'S A FINE ART TO BEING A GODLY HELPMATE. It's a well-crafted blend of encouragement, correction, counsel, support, and respect. It's beautiful to behold in any season of life, but it is truly breathtaking to observe when the storms of life hit. That's what I saw when my friend Grace went through one of the most turbulent periods of her twenty-one-year marriage to Frank. Her story should provide hope to others who find themselves in difficult times, tempted to bolt, and unsure if God will provide the help, support, and strength needed to maintain a difficult marriage.

New Year's Day had dawned sunny and bright. Grace Carver smiled to herself as she took down the holiday decorations. The past few Christmases had been nomadic and chaotic, but this Christmas had been peaceful in their new home. Grace savored the memories of her growing family's celebration and looked forward to creating more in the coming year.

The next day, bad news dashed her hopes to the hard floor, like delicate Christmas ornaments shattered into dozens of brightly colored shards. Her husband—a man often commended by their pastors and a lay leader within their church—had been arrested for embezzling and released on his own recognizance.

When Frank told her the news, he hung his head in humiliation, tears coursing down his cheeks. In shock, Grace stared at her husband, unable at first to voice her thoughts. Lots of seemingly unrelated memories washed over her and snapped into place as the reality of this news set in. The new electronics in the house. The bank errands he always seemed eager to do. The vague answers to the questions she raised about his erratic schedule. With the clarity of hindsight, her mind then raced into the future. Frank had a high profile in his industry and was considered a leader in his field nationally. Would this arrest make the press? Would the children hear about it? Would he be able to keep his job? Would they be able to stay in their new home?

To her dismay, the news trucks were already gathering out front. Soon Frank's face and the account of his arrest began churning through the media matrix. People who had never met him but associated him with the negative corporate reputation of his employer soon were slandering him on their blogs and personal websites. Unable to bear the burden of scandal, his employer terminated him immediately. But Frank maintained it was all a misunderstanding and it would soon be straightened out.

The first night, neither Frank nor Grace could sleep. They sat up in bed, weeping and holding hands. As Grace watched her glowing alarm clock record the creeping minutes between midnight and dawn, a memory from a prayer meeting several months prior suddenly came to mind. At this meeting, she and Frank had been prayed over by several pastors, and one had a specific impression while they prayed. This pastor told Grace he sensed there was a storm coming—a serious trial in their future. But he assured them God would have His people in every place to help them. Then this pastor reminded Grace that she was called to be a keeper in their home to provide peace and normality in the midst of the storm. Grace had simply recorded this impression in her prayer journal—a scrapbook overflowing with greeting cards, Scripture verses, and other tokens of God's faithfulness—but didn't worry about it.

Now these words brought comfort in the bleak darkness of night. Grace knew what she was to be doing in the coming days. Unlike Job's wife, her counsel to Frank would not be "curse God and die" but rather "praise God and live." She began to meditate on how much God must really love Frank to expose this deception and not let the consequences of sin multiply.

The next day, longtime friends gathered at the Carvers' home. Frank was shell-shocked and Grace alternated between fear, faith, and grief. Two longtime ministry friends called to offer their support and prayers—and their specific encouragement to Grace: "We're praying for you, that you would see this crisis in the perspective of a lifelong marriage. We are asking God to give you the wisdom to make decisions today in light of the years yet to come in your marriage."

Later that day, Frank met with his senior pastor. Grace was surprised by how long he was gone. When Frank returned, he slipped quietly upstairs to their room without saying anything to her or the children. Moments later, the phone rang. It was their pastor.

"Grace, I want you to know that you can call me at any time," he said. "I believe there is more to be revealed about this situation and God is going to use you in that process. You are going to have to ask Frank some questions.

You will need to lovingly confront him and not coddle him. Care for him, yes. Coddle his pride, no. I believe the Holy Spirit will give you the wisdom to know the difference."

As it turned out, Grace had plenty of time to practice. Despite Frank's initial protestations of innocence, the legal proceedings against him continued for several months. More charges were filed, more lawyers were hired, more articles were published. And Grace grew more skilled in drawing out her husband.

"I knew my role was to speak truth to him," she recalls. "But I didn't know exactly what to do. When I spoke to our pastor, he would say, 'Don't allow him to talk about a lot of superficial things just to fill up the time. You need to ask him questions, such as how is your soul? What are you thinking about?' We never had fellowship before at this level. Of course, in the past we talked and prayed together, but I had never asked him questions like these. My role was to go where I didn't necessarily want to go, to pursue him, to ask questions—and then to not let sin-minimizing words hide the truth. We had to learn to use biblical words, to use God's words to identify sin and to recognize His sanctifying grace at work in us both. I soon learned that sometimes I was supposed to confront Frank, but other times I was just supposed to lovingly walk alongside of a man who was limping."

Through the skillful care of his pastor and the encouraging ministry of his wife, Frank eventually confessed that the charges against him were accurate and he began the process of restitution. By the time his court date arrived, the state's attorney and his own lawyers had worked out a plea agreement in which Frank would plead guilty—rightfully acknowledging his sin—but receive probation before judgment. The judge agreed to the terms and Frank walked out of that courtroom with the opportunity for a successful probation period to wipe clean his legal record. He remains a fruitful member in their church, serving in several ministries, and is gainfully employed once again.

Looking back, Grace says their deep friendship helped to anchor their marriage during the crisis. Because she loved and respected Frank, she did not battle significant bitterness or self-righteousness. More importantly, her own relationship with the Lord equipped her to withstand the howling winds of crisis.

"As helpmates, we need to be independent in our faith," Grace says. "We have this idea that we're kind of leaning on our husbands for everything, but if we are truly women of God, then we have to be independent in pursuing Him and making our spiritual roots go down deep to withstand the storms. There will be seasons where we'll be the ones called to support our husbands or family members during a crisis. I think wives need to learn how to be that to our husbands. I think of the Marines and how they say you never leave a man behind—as believers, that's what we have to do. We have to go back and get those who are wounded and sinning and get them to safety."

Five

THERE'S NO
Place Like Home

*W*riting this book, I spent a lot of time in my house, staring at the walls as I tried to collect my thoughts. Like many people, I often work at home. The home as work space gets a fair amount of attention these days as more people start home-based businesses or telecommute from home. You may assume this is a new trend, but it's actually a very old idea. As we'll see in this chapter, the history of the home is actually a lot more convoluted than we might understand today. The history of domesticity is relevant to the ongoing feminist discussion about where women should invest their time and energy. I didn't even know the half of it as I started my research—I was completely fascinated to learn about the golden age of domesticity, the real roots of home economics, and how consumer marketing has shaped much of our culture's assessment of the home. Nevertheless, Scripture is very clear that wisdom or folly is demonstrated by how a woman treats her home. "The wise woman builds her house, but with her own hands the foolish one tears hers down" (Proverbs 14:1 NIV).

IT ALL BEGAN WITH A FEW phone calls to some elite brides in the New York area.

Feminist author and lawyer Linda Hirshman was researching a book on marriage after feminism, and she expected these fortysomething women—the logical heirs of the feminist movement—would reflect the substantial changes of the feminist movement in their lives. Instead, she discovered, what was for her, an unpleasant surprise:

> Ninety percent of the brides I found had had babies. Of the thirty with babies, five were still working full time. Twenty-five, or 85 percent, were not working full time. Of those not working full time, ten were working part time but often a long way from their prior career paths. And half the married women with children were not working at all.[1]

This survey led to Hirshman's infamous article in the November 2005 edition of the *American Prospect* called "Homeward Bound." In this piece, Hirshman railed at "choice feminism," saying it was no real choice for women to leave the workplace for the sake of their families because the "real glass ceiling was at home." In this article, she wrote that women were making bad choices because feminism *wasn't radical enough.* "It changed the workplace but it didn't change men, and, more importantly, it didn't fundamentally change how women related to men," she wrote.[2]

Hirshman believes that "choice feminism" is no credible form of feminism at all. In her view, feminists made headway in the marketplace but failed to transform the family. "In interviews, women with enough money to quit work say they are 'choosing' to opt out,'" she writes. "Their words conceal a crucial reality: the belief that women are responsible for child-rearing and homemaking was largely untouched by decades of workplace feminism."[3]

Her book, *Get to Work*, was released shortly thereafter. It expanded upon the theme of the "Homeward Bound" article with more pointed critique:

Bounding home is not good for women and it's not good for the society. The women aren't using their capacities fully; their so-called free choice makes them unfree dependents on their husbands. Whether they leave the workplace altogether or just cut back on their commitment, their talent and education are lost from the public world to the private world of laundry and kissing boo-boos. The abandonment of the public world by women at the top means the ruling class is overwhelmingly male. If the rulers are male, they will make mistakes that benefit males. Picture an all-male Supreme Court. We may well go back there. What will that mean for the women of America?[4]

For six months, the media controversy continued to boil. Then the *Washington Post* gave Hirshman the opportunity to write a rebuttal piece, "Unleashing the Wrath of Stay at-Home Moms." As we've seen in the writing of many feminists among all three waves, the real offense to feminists is not a dissenting opinion but dissenting *Bible-based* opinion, something that seemed to be of paramount importance for Hirshman to note:

I learned something people really need to know. The aggressive domesticity is not coming only from a bunch of women who can't manage all the demands on their time. Time and again, when I could identify the sources of the most rabid criticism and Google them, male and female, they had fundamentalist religious stuff on their Web sites or in the involuntary biographies that Google makes possible. A lot of the fundamentalism behind the stay-at-home mom movement is overt, such as the letters worrying about my soul that appeared after the head of the Southern Baptist Theological Seminary suggested his followers chat me up. But a lot of it is covert, such as the identity of the authors of manuals disguised as tips on frugal housekeeping, but actually proselytizing women to stay home, as the Bible suggests.[5]

What Hirshman stirred up with her articles and her resulting book is really a two-pronged debate. The first is the value of the home versus the value of the marketplace. That's what we'll explore in this chapter. The second is the definition and practice of motherhood. The much vaunted "mommy wars" will be the topic of the following chapter. In some ways, they are interchangeable, but we'll start with home, sweet home.

Hirshman's analysis reflects the social upheaval that began at the end of the 18th century. Though in 1963 Betty Friedan wrote of the "trapped housewife syndrome," she did not make a unique discovery, either. The bifurcation of the public and private spheres, the economic analysis of housewives as "unfree dependents," and the market valuation of child care are discussions that began in first-wave feminism. For a brief, shining moment there was an opportunity to honor and value the home and those who labor in it. But it was lost, trampled by a myriad of factors stemming from the rise of democracy to the Industrial Revolution and on to the culture of consumerism. These historical factors, which we'll explore in the coming pages, contributed to the disdain for the biblical perspective on the home.

Even so, God's Word provides this timeless, unchanging exhortation: "The wise woman builds her house, but with her own hands the foolish one tears hers down" (Proverbs 14:1 NIV).

Wisdom and folly await as we explore the history of the home.

Simple Shelter

In the 1980s, trend forecaster Faith Popcorn coined the term "cocooning." She defined it as the tendency to retreat to the home for personal comfort and sanctuary. Since 1950, the average U.S. home has grown from an average of 983 square feet to 2266 square feet in 2000, more than doubling as the number of residents decreased.[6] New homes often have a full bathroom for each occupant, a home theater, an outdoor entertainment space, and a showcase kitchen that can accommodate a crowd of people and appliances. "All the comforts of home" took on a new meaning in the last few decades.

Home wasn't always such a collection of creature comforts, though. In fact, for most of recorded history, the bulk of humanity lived in simple dwellings. Except for the wealthy and the ruling class, most everyone's homes in antiquity were utilitarian, rather than monuments to personal style and taste.

Let's start with the kind of home Abraham gave up to go where God would lead him. When Abraham walked the narrow streets of Ur, he would only have passed doors. Homes then did not have windows. The doors opened into a central courtyard, around which other rooms were built. The courtyard was the only source of interior daylight. Ur was a sophisticated city, so many middle-class homes had two stories. A house typically measured forty by fifty feet and had ten to twenty tiny rooms, many for storage. The first floor had areas for cooking (usually done in the open courtyard) and dining, as well as storage and a rudimentary lavatory. The second floor was where the family slept. All the doorways had brick sills or thresholds to keep the rainwater and waste from flowing into the house. The street level often rose over time, too, as uncollected garbage accumulated there.[7]

The furniture in these homes was equally simple, even sparse. People generally sat on a cushion on the floor or on a stool. There were some simple tables and possibly a brick bench that served as a "sofa" during the day and a "bed" at night, when the bedroll was unfolded. However, most people slept on a bedroll on the floor. Indoor lights were simple saucer oil lamps with flax wicks.[8]

By the time the nomadic Hebrews settled in Canaan and began to live once again in houses, they typically lived in four-room structures built around an open courtyard. The doorway led to an open courtyard with tamped-down earth, with a room on one side for storage and a room on the other side for a mule or cow, and a back room for sleeping. The rooms were small and often only had pillars, instead of walls, dividing the areas. The courtyard had a fire pit, serving as the kitchen and dining area. As in Abraham's time, the houses were essentially windowless and the doors were simple wooden doors that could be barred shut. These homes had essentially no furniture. Sometimes they had a stone bench to sit on or unfold a bedroll.[9]

The home may not have been a place of luxury, but it was a place of community. Though men and women had different tasks, they generally labored together in the same vicinity. Men were largely responsible for animal husbandry (they raised sheep in large numbers), farming, and pottery production—most of their dishes were made from clay and fired in a rudimentary kiln. Women were largely responsible for caring for the children and making clothing and food, though they did work in the fields seasonally. Bread was made from hand-ground grain and baked in small mud brick or pottery ovens, placed on a fire with hot stones underneath. The women also cooked one-pot meals of vegetables and grains over an open fire.[10]

Though they had to produce what they ate or needed, the Hebrews were able to develop additional materials with which to barter or trade. Twice a year, they sheared their sheep. The sheep were washed in a pool before they were sheared; afterward, the women washed the sheared wool again and combed it out. Then these women prepared the wool for spinning and weaving, and created the cloth for their wardrobe. Any extra wool also served as "cash crop"—an item for trading that could supplement a family's income.[11]

This four-room house persisted as the basic design of Israelite homes through the united monarchy all the way to the destruction of Jerusalem by the Babylonians in 586 BC. Their furniture remained essentially the same too. While monarchs such as Saul, David, or Solomon might have dined seated at a low table, most poor people spread an animal skin on the ground and ate their food off of it. The conditions were extremely unsanitary as well. Human excrement was usually buried in a "waste field," but the streets were strewn with animal manure and other garbage.

Despite these modest settings, hospitality was essential throughout Hebrew history. The host was expected to provide his best for any guest, and the head of the home washed the feet of strangers, which signaled the host's care and protection of the guest. (And maybe it was practical, too, considering what everyone was trampling in those streets!) Hospitality was considered inviolable in Semitic society as a whole—which explains (but does not excuse) some of the difficult passages in the Bible where guests were treated much better than family members.[12]

Those are the practical matters, but what did it mean for women in Old Testament times? According to *The New Illustrated Bible Manners and Customs*, Hebrew women were respected even though they had different roles and tasks in the home and community:

> Child-bearing remained the primary responsibility of the mother or
> wife, who had the authority to manage the household. She rationed and
> allocated food supplies, prepared food and processed and stored it. She
> served as administrator with economic responsibilities as she managed

the "family budget," and judicial responsibilities as she adjudicated responsibilities within the household. And while the father or patriarch designated an heir, the mother often exercised the power (note Bathsheba's role in the selection of Solomon to be king). The mother taught the children. This is an important point to keep in mind when we think of all the pagan women in Solomon's harem—incapable of bringing up children in the ways of God and thus contributing to the rise of idolatry. When boys became young men, fathers took over the responsibility for their education, but mothers continued the responsibility of teaching girls after they became young women. Although women often helped out with herding and farming, the primary responsibility for such activity rested with the men.

In modern feminist discussion the assumption is often made that women in ancient Israel had inferior roles. But the women in Hebrew households had a status equal to or greater than the status of many men. And the biblical pattern is to honor one's "father *and* mother" (e.g., Exodus 20:12; 2 Samuel 19:37; Proverbs 15:20). Honoring involved respect, deference to, obedience to, and caring for in old age or adverse circumstances in a society that had no social security provisions.[13]

Women were also educated. By the end of the eighth century BC, Israelite society was largely literate. The Hebrew alphabet, consisting of only twenty-two letters, made widespread literacy much easier than in Egypt or Mesopotamia with their hundreds of hieroglyphics and cuneiform signs.[14] Because female literacy rates are often a window into the value of women in any given culture or society, it is a reflection of their essential equality in worth and value that Hebrew women were literate and bore the main responsibility for educating their children.

What an important point to remember the next time someone points out how women in Bible times were oppressed!

The New Testament Home

By the time Jesus walked around Galilee, not a great deal had changed regarding the structure of the home. Except for the wealthy, homes were about the same size and still furnished quite simply, though it was increasingly popular to use the roof for a myriad of purposes, including sleeping in hot weather, drying fruit and flax, and praying. The poor still slept on bedrolls, usually made of straw, and sat on the floor to eat. But in this period, nearly all classes had some furniture—stools, chairs with backs, low dining tables, and beds with slats or ropes to support a mattress. The upper classes reclined on couches while dining, with their heads supported on their left elbow, while they ate with their right hands. Their feet were pointed away from the table, just as it was described in Matthew 26:6–13 when a woman—thought to be Mary—anointed the feet of Jesus as He dined in her home.[15]

In the New Testament era, Palestine had become more urbanized. Town industry became more common, with practiced craft occupations such as tailors, cobblers, masons, stonecutters, carpenters, bakers, perfumers, butchers, weavers, potters, doctors, scribes, and more. Workers in the same crafts tended to live near each other in town, like rudimentary guilds.[16] Due to being part of the Roman Empire, trade had increased significantly. Therefore, there was a great range of goods available to the average housewife on market day—traditionally held on Friday, the day before the Sabbath. Because it was a "Day of Assembly," Friday was also the day for public occasions such as weddings or legal hearings.[17]

Similar activities were seen in the homes of women in Greece and Asia Minor as the New Testament church expanded. Women, assisted by household bond servants, produced wool thread and did some weaving at home. Even commercial textile producers then did not do much spinning or weaving.[18] In Greek households, such as in Corinth, wives supervised the household property, male and female servants, the kitchen, the nursing of the sick, the production of clothes, and the rearing of the children.

In a nutshell, the wife controlled all domestic activities.[19]

The Ways of Her Household

This is the cultural background for the various passages we find in the Scriptures about the home. Though it may have been modest in comparison to the minipalaces of the modern age, the home remained important in the Scriptures. In fact, in the Psalms we find two verses that speak specifically of the blessings of home.

God settles the solitary in a home; he leads out the prisoners to prosperity, but the rebellious dwell in a parched land. (Psalm 68:6)
He gives the barren woman a home, making her the joyous mother of children. Praise the Lord! (Psalm 113:9)

One way God chooses to bless people is by providing a home—a haven in a harsh world and a place where relationships can thrive and be fruitful. And a barren woman who is now settled in her home to care for her children is a praiseworthy item, according to the Bible, not an object of pity or scorn. Additionally, we see that one of the last things Jesus did was to make sure His mother was provided for by John, His disciple: "Then he said to the disciple, 'Behold, your mother!' *And from that hour the disciple took her to his own home*" (John 19:27, emphasis added).

That paragon of wisdom and virtue, the Proverbs 31 woman, also exemplified domestic wisdom by running a home that was a blessing to all connected to it. The many verses that commend her activities are summed up in verse 27, "She looks well to the ways of her household and does not eat the bread of idleness." In contrast, the harlot described earlier in Proverbs does *not* tend to her home. "And behold, the woman meets him, dressed as a prostitute, wily of heart. She is loud and wayward; her feet do not stay at home; now in the street, now in the market, and at every corner she lies in wait" (Proverbs 7:10–12).

This contrast in virtue is the reason the apostle Paul instructs Christian women not to neglect their homes. Titus 2:3–5 says, "Older women likewise are to be reverent in behavior, not slanderers or slaves to much wine. They are to teach what is good, and so train the young women to love their husbands and children, to be self-controlled, pure, working at home, kind, and submissive to their own husbands, that the word of God may not be reviled."

It's easy to understand why self-control, kindness, and purity are essential to protecting the Word of God, not to mention loving family relationships. It's not always immediately apparent how homemaking can be meaningful in the big picture of the gospel, though. Homemaking is simply the collection of tasks that keep a home running. These tasks are no more the ultimate definition of "looking well to the ways of a household" than cleaning out electronic files, deleting email, answering the phone, and booking travel reservations are to the actual definition of office work. Every sphere has its repetitive tasks that contribute to the larger goal of productivity.

The point of being a keeper at home is to provide a haven for a godly family to thrive (a requirement for church leadership, according to 1 Timothy 3:1–5), to offer hospitality to fellow Christians and non-Christians alike, and to provide a place for the church to meet. Even though the early church met primarily in homes, even today our homes can operate as an extension of the larger Sunday gathering when we meet in small groups or Bible studies. Hospitality remains a command for all believers throughout the ages—"Contribute to the needs of the saints and seek to show hospitality" (Romans 12:13).

However, even among a large number of Christians today, the home is not as important as it once was, nor is it viewed as a place of ministry and outreach. This is a result of a collision of trends in the mid-nineteenth century that tarnished domesticity and led to feminism's vitriolic attack against the home.

Republican Motherhood

The highly segregated spheres of home and workplace are a relatively new development in human history—a legacy of the Industrial Revolution in the nineteenth century. Author and professor Nancy Pearcey says modern champions of the family will not understand the diminished importance of the home until they take into account the demise of the family's economic base. She writes:

> Prior to the 19th century, the vast majority of people in the world lived on farms or in peasant villages. Productive work was done in the home or its outbuildings, whether for subsistence or for sale. Work was done not by individuals, but by families. Stores, offices, and workshops were located in a front room, with living quarters either upstairs or in the rear. The boundaries of the home were fluid and permeable; the "world" entered continually in the form of clients, business colleagues, customers, and apprentices.
> What did this integration of work and life mean for family relationships? For husband and wife, it meant they inhabited the same

universe, working side by side in a common enterprise (though not necessarily in identical tasks). For the mother, the location of work within the home meant she was able to raise children while still participating in the family sustenance. Marriage in colonial times "meant to become a co-worker beside a husband, if necessary learning new skills in butchering, silversmith work, printing, or upholstering—whatever special skills the husband's work required." Of course, women were also responsible for household tasks which required a wide range of skills: spinning wool and cotton; weaving it into cloth; sewing the family's clothes; gardening and preserving food; preparing meals without pre-processed ingredients; making soap, buttons, candles, medicines. Colonial mothers did not need to start a feminist movement to demand a role in economically productive work. Many of the goods used in colonial society were manufactured by women, doing the brainwork (planning and managing) as well as the handwork.

Fathers enjoyed the same integration of work and child rearing responsibilities. Parenting was not, as today, almost exclusively the mother's domain. Sermons, child-rearing manuals, and other prescriptive literature of the day addressed both parents, admonishing them to "raise up" their children together. When manuals did address one parent, it was usually the father, who was thought to be particularly important in religious and intellectual training. With productive endeavor centered on the family hearth, fathers were "a visible presence, year after year, day after day." They trained their children to work alongside them. "Fatherhood was thus an extension, if not an integral part, of much routine activity."[20]

The Industrial Revolution and the increased urbanization of our new nation drastically altered what had been the status quo for centuries. However, it wasn't just these two factors that affected the home. The formation of this new political experiment called the United States of America also profoundly affected the home. At first that was a good thing, says historian Glenna Matthews, author of *"Just a Housewife": The Rise and Fall of Domesticity in America*:

Perhaps the most important factor in elevating the status of the home was the role home played in the polity after the American Revolution.

In fact, the intermingling of the domestic and the political began even earlier than the war itself, with the boycott of British-made goods. What had been viewed by men and women alike as a set of petty concerns—the kind of cloth to be employed in making a suit, for example—acquired a whole new political relevance. The boycotts would not have worked without the cooperation of women acting within their own households, and this gave women a new self-respect and a rationale for entering into political discussions. . . .

But it was the widespread concern over how best to socialize citizens after the war that had the largest impact. There were no precedents for a republic on the scale of the United States. Many people believed that the new nation would require the support of a uniquely public-spirited citizenry. If citizens must learn to place a high value on the public interest, this was a lesson they would need to begin in childhood. Thus the home became crucial to the success of the nation and women—whose education began to be taken much more seriously than ever before—gained the role of "Republican Mother." . . .[21]

The ideology of Republican Motherhood was a significant reason for the sharp increase in American women's literacy rates. By 1860, there was little discernible difference between male and female literacy.[22] The Republican Motherhood concept also began to spill out of the home into the public square as women championed the idea that concern for the home should translate into concern for the culture. The charitable energies of the home began to overflow to society as women organized benevolent agencies to combat drunkenness, slavery, gambling, and other evils of the age.

It was the beginning of the golden age of domesticity.

The Golden Age of Domesticity

As the Industrial Revolution pulled more and more men into factories and offices, the contrast between the competitive world of manufacturing and capitalism created a longing for the "haven of home" as a counterbalance—a place of refuge for the weary worker. Industry also improved the home, with new inventions such as the cast-iron stove, sewing machine, and other appliances that made domesticity more interesting and less arduous. Thus, as the workplace became increasingly mechanized and impersonal, the home became more refined, serving as the outpost for the intangible qualities that improved society. The resulting intense focus on the home became known as the "cult of domesticity" or the "golden age of domesticity."

Many books and magazines of the time promoted the ideal home with vigor, and no one did it better than Sarah Josepha Hale. She was the editor of *Godey's Lady's Book*, one of the first women's magazines. At its peak of popularity, it had a circulation of 150,000. Historian Glenna Matthews says that, unquestionably, Hale was one of the two or three most influential American women of the nineteenth century. We are living with her influence even today—every time we sit down for Thanksgiving dinner. Matthews notes how Hale was persistent in campaigning for this holiday:

> No feminist by modern standards—she opposed woman suffrage and believed in clearly delineated separate spheres for the two sexes—Hale was nonetheless a forceful advocate of many improvements in woman's status. She campaigned for better education for women, including higher education. She campaigned for the admission of women to the medical profession. She campaigned for property rights for married women. The list of her favorite reforms would be a long one. Moreover, despite her aversion to women casting ballots, she did not draw the line at other forms of political activity such as writing letters to politicians. Indeed, in the pursuit of her most cherished goal of having the President set aside a national Thanksgiving Day, she fired off a constant barrage of letters to governors, senators, secretaries of state, and Presidents. . . . In 1863, President Lincoln rewarded her efforts on behalf of Thanksgiving Day by proclaiming it as a national holiday. This was an open acknowledgment not only of Hale's influence but also of the political ramifications of domesticity, because Hale had based her campaign for the holiday on the political benefits to be derived from a feast in which the whole nation could participate at once.[23]

Hale wasn't the only one wielding her pen to affect politics. An occasional contributor to *Godey's* went on to publish a book that transformed the nation—*Uncle Tom's Cabin*. Harriet Beecher Stowe wrote this novel to express her outrage over the passage of the Fugitive Slave Act of 1850. Precisely because it was written in the golden age of domesticity, Stowe had the pluck to boldly target slavery through the lens of domestic values. Matthews says many things were remarkable about the timing of this book:

> First, American novelists had been—almost to a person—silent on the subject of slavery up to 1851. Second, although women writers were tapping a vast market with the domestic novel, there were few attempting to write on public issues for a general audience. . . . Finally, Stowe, though the member of an accomplished family, had no reason to think of herself as destined for a public role.[24]

> The novel is a stunning achievement because it combines moral and religious passion with the realistic detail of a genre painting. Stowe wanted to replace the sordid, unchristian, money-grubbing values of the marketplace and the accommodationist politics of those who voted for the Fugitive Slave Act with a new set of values based on true Christianity and love. But rather than a utopian approach to what could replace the status quo, she had a very practical vision, which was the set of values and behavior to be found in a loving Christian home presided over by a large-hearted woman. In the words of Jane Tompkins, "the popular domestic novel of the nineteenth century represents a monumental effort to reorganize culture from the woman's point of view," and *Uncle Tom's Cabin* is the "summa theologica" of this effort.[25]

With women becoming more active in reform societies and charitable organizations, their energies gave rise to the progressive era that blossomed in the nineteenth century. As Pearcey writes, to reform the public sphere, women began to work through the church in the name of Christian benevolence:

> They joined or started societies to feed and clothe the poor. They supported the Sunday school movement and missionary societies. They joined or founded organizations to abolish slavery, to outlaw prostitution and abortion, to stop public drunkenness and gambling. They supported orphan asylums and societies such as the YWCA to assist single

women in the cities. They initiated movements to abolish child labor, establish juvenile courts, and strengthen food and drug laws. This interlocking network of reform societies has been dubbed the Benevolent Empire. . . . But most of these early crusaders were definitely *not* feminists: They did not base their claim to work outside the home on the feminist argument that there are no important differences between men and women. Just the opposite: They accepted the doctrine that women are more loving, more sensitive, more pious—but then they argued that it was *precisely those qualities* that equipped them for benevolent work beyond the confines of the home.[26]

Though the golden age of domesticity seemed to afford women high respect, it actually set the stage for the dawning of feminism. As Pearcey observes, making women the guardians of morality—the enforcers of male virtue—led to a diminished definition of masculinity. "For the first time, moral and spiritual leadership were no longer viewed as masculine attributes. They became women's work," she writes. "[Men] were becoming content with a stunted definition of masculinity as tough, competitive, and pragmatic, which denied their moral and spiritual aspirations."[27] And as she notes, this had severe repercussions on the church, as well:

Where was the Christian church in all this? Did it stand firmly against the "demoralization" of the male character? Sadly, no. Instead the American church largely acquiesced in the redefinition of masculinity. After centuries of teaching that husbands and fathers were divinely called to the office of household headship, the church began to pitch its appeal primarily to women. Churchmen began to speak of women as having a special gift for religion and morality. . . . In short, instead of challenging the growing secularism among men, the church largely acquiesced—by turning to women. Churchmen seemed relieved to find at least one sphere, the home, where religion still held sway.[28]

The golden age of domesticity was a short one, though, because a new theory was brewing—one that would demean women and the home in unprecedented ways.

Social Darwinism and Home Economics

With the rise of the female-driven Benevolent Empire, it's no surprise that eventually many men came to resent the perceived female hegemony over virtue and the women reformers' attempts to control masculine vices. Their rescue, so to speak, came when Charles Darwin promoted evolutionary theory in his 1859 publication *On the Origin of Species*. This book really hurt the cause of women because Darwin viewed women as lesser beings in the system of evolution. Matthews says that according to a number of sources, Darwin was not very enlightened about women, even though he had married his cousin and fathered ten children. She adds:

> Darwinism tended to be reductionist with respect to women, making reproductive capacity the chief criterion of female excellence. Hence, the whole complex of moral, social, and religious values associated with Republican Motherhood was cast in shadow. Moreover, Darwin and many of his followers explicitly stated that women are biologically inferior to men. This, too, had a negative impact on the status of the home. Perhaps most damaging to the home was the fact that Darwin's theory of sexual selection located the source of evolutionary change in male struggle for mates, making men and male activity the "vanguard of evolution." Finally, Darwin helped promote the secularization of American society, and thus served further to undermine the religious role of the home. All of this eroded the interest of American intellectuals, including women, in domesticity.[29]

His ideas were immediately incorporated into what's been called Social Darwinism, the belief that only the strongest or fittest should survive and flourish in society, while the weak and unfit should be allowed to die. In the nineteenth century, Social Darwinists said that the reason men were superior to women was that, since the dawn of time, men had fought for survival in the world, where they were honed by competition and natural selection. In comparison, women were sheltered from this process because they were at home with the children—thus, they evolved more slowly. Even those who tried to defend women against this idea only helped with faint praise: women weren't inherently inferior, but their confinement to the home left them with undeveloped or stunted mental faculties.

One prominent feminist (ironically, the great-niece of Harriet Beecher Stowe) managed to build upon Social Darwinism to question the competence of homemakers everywhere. By the turn of the century, the forceful Charlotte Perkins Gilman, author of *Women and Economics* and the classic feminist novella *The Yellow Wallpaper*, had greatly devalued the home as it was celebrated in the antebellum period, the golden age of domesticity. She argued that women's confinement to the home was the main reason for female inferiority. Therefore, her solution was to professionalize it. "The home of the future is one in which not one stroke of work shall be done except by professional people who are paid by the hour," she wrote.[30]

Gilman's impact on domesticity was enormous. As Matthews says, "Building on evolutionary theory, she probably did more to separate the home from history, that is, to make the home seem to be a retrograde and irrelevant institution, than any other individual. . . . If educated men reflected about the home at all, there was the reassuring thought that a new discipline, home economics, had come into being to solve domestic difficulties."[31]

Ah, home economics. It sounds so earnestly pop culture—a dim memory from middle school in the heyday of the 1960s or 1970s—doesn't it? Actually, despite that awkward teenage classroom experience, the concept of home economics stretches back to the beginning of the twentieth century—where we find Charlotte Perkins Gilman. Gilman wanted to both free women from the constraints of the home *and* apply scientific and business principles to modernize domesticity through the new field of home economics. As Matthews notes:

> When we come to Gilman, however, we come to one whose loathing for the home limited her ability to envision how domesticity and justice for women could be compatible. Moreover, she shared Darwin's low estimation of the female contribution to human progress. Indeed, the two attributes were not unrelated. It was because she saw so little positive in "home-making," insisting that what traditionally have been women's tasks are not truly productive, that she could dismiss female contributions so readily: . . . "We are the only animal species in which

the female depends on the male for food, the only animal species in which the sex-relation is also an economic relation." . . .

Not only did Darwinism help to shape her estimate of woman's work, but evolution also explained the primitive nature of the home in her view. Rather than equating antiquity with value, she equated it with datedness: the home is our oldest institution and perforce the lowest and most out-of-date.[32]

So in come the early home economists, hoping that sanitary science and public health would be the centerpiece of urban reform. Eager to apply the latest business and scientific principles to the home, these new home economists thought they were creating a place for women in science. What they ended up creating, however, was the ultimate consumer.

Marketing to Mrs. Consumer

One of the most famous home economists was Christine Frederick, who passionately promoted the concept of the scientific management model for home economics. She had her degree in science from Northwestern University and had married and given birth to four children before she began to study kitchen efficiency. She set up a model kitchen in her home—known as the Applecroft Home Experiment Station—and began to experiment there with efficiency studies. Her experiments became famous, leading to a position as the household editor for the *Ladies Home Journal*. Today, whatever attracts a lot of attention soon finds advertisers hovering nearby; such was also the case with Frederick's model kitchen, says Matthews.

In the years between 1913 and 1929, Frederick moved from being a pioneering home economist to being a pioneering advertising woman. As her Applecroft Home Experiment Station became well known, manufacturers began to send her their products to test. If the product in question met with her approval, she would write promotional literature on its behalf, evidently never worrying about what this did to her credibility as an unbiased expert. Because in its infancy the advertising industry discriminated against women, she founded the League of Advertising Women in New York in 1912 and gave increasing time and attention to this pursuit. . . . Frederick's metamorphosis is indicative of the ease with which corporate America would be able to "buy" home economists as spokeswomen, thereby undermining the independence of the discipline. . . . Moreover, the field was misconceived because it is impossible to "help" a housewife while systematically disparaging her life experiences and judgment. . . . Finally, when efficiency, expertise, and fidelity to the scientific method become the highest values, the ability to resist a good offer from an advertiser is greatly undermined. If the home is important because it is outside the cash nexus, because it celebrates values in opposition to marketplace values . . . then there might be a reason to say no to General Foods or General Mills. In parting company with this tradition, the home economists in essence made ready to perform the role of Betty Crocker and the rest of her sisterhood.[33]

Frederick went on to write *Selling Mrs. Consumer*, a book aimed at the advertising industry that delineated how to get housewives to spend as much as possible. Because industrial capitalism is fueled by a high level of consumer spending, this task was assigned to women. Soon magazines such as the *Ladies Home Journal* were carrying the banner for the new consumer home, publishing articles about the latest electrical appliances, the new food substitutes, and the latest home goods.

Thus the shift from the home as a place of production to a place of consumption was completed. In the new culture of consumption—bolstered by the age of advertising and the push for consumer credit—all vestiges of nineteenth-century concerns with character, self-restraint, and sacrifice were gone. Republican Motherhood had been replaced with Mrs. Consumer. The Benevolent Empire was replaced with the hedonistic attitude of the "Jazz Age" of the 1920s. While women celebrated their new freedom to vote, first-wave feminism came to a close, and the nation turned its attention to the growing problems of fascism and socialism looming in Europe.

The following decades were a struggle for survival. The Great Depression and World War II sobered the nation, but the war effort also pushed nearly six million women into the workforce. Some even hinted then that a housewife was not filling her patriotic duty. A columnist for the *Detroit Free Press*, for example, stated that a housewife should surrender her seat on a bus to a woman war worker.[34] The impact of Rosie the Riveter is legendary—and volumes have already been written about this iconic war image—so I will not pursue that here. What I do want to highlight is that the postwar period created both a nation ready for a respite and a sizable subculture of radical activists involved in communism, socialism, and labor politics. Both factors contributed to the rise of second-wave feminism.

Many of us have seen the patronizing advertising and articles churned out in the 1950s. Home as portrayed in media and advertising then was a place full of technological marvels that caused rapturous swooning in grown women. Mrs. Consumer was back—and better than ever. As Matthews notes, "After the privations of depression and war, early marriage and large families had come into fashion. The grim events of the preceding twenty years had made it difficult to believe in the individual's capacity to have a positive influence on his or her society. Therefore, the home once more became a haven, but an apolitical one, unlike the home of the antebellum years. In an age of anxiety engendered by the Cold War and the nuclear threat, the chief quality desired of women was that they be soothing."[35]

It was in the postwar period that Betty Friedan began her writing career. The woman who would make the malaise of the housewife a national concern in the 1960s with the publication of *The Feminine Mystique* was actually a product of the Communist-Socialist politics she embraced in the 1940s and 1950s. Though she maintained that she had been a typical suburban housewife, her biographer, historian Daniel Horowitz, says she was far from typical; rather, she had been a political activist involved in Communist politics and freelance writing for twenty-five years before she published *The Feminine Mystique*. Her political views collided with the media and advertising machine of the 1950s, a time when marketing to Mrs. Consumer was in all its patronizing glory. In *The Feminine Mystique*, Friedan challenged the 1950s ideal of female fulfillment through marriage, motherhood, and suburban domesticity by calling the suburban home a "comfortable concentration camp."

The Heart of the Home

So here we are in the twenty-first century, reaping the harvest of all these changes and ideas. Friedan's writing shaped the debate that is still brewing today in Linda Hirshman's battle against "choice feminism" and women who "opt out" of the workforce to stay at home. The same public sphere–private sphere dichotomy that arose nearly two hundred years ago colors our thinking today. If we are wise, we will comprehend the economic values that created this dichotomy and continue to permeate our culture's thinking. If we are honest, we will also acknowledge that what advertising promises in terms of satisfaction in material goods is an empty promise and that feminists are partially right in rebelling against the mind-numbing consumerism pitched at women. No one will find fulfillment in the latest appliances or gadgets that run a home. Nor will one find lasting fulfillment in attempting to decorate and entertain like the latest hospitality doyenne. Material goods and self-glorifying domestic perfectionism are definitely not the heart of the home.

The heart of the home is found in the relationships nurtured there and the comfort offered to one another—comfort we have first received from God, the Father of compassion, and then share with one another (2 Corinthians 1:3–4). Home is no lesser sphere, for Scripture says it must be built by divine wisdom (Proverbs 14:1; 24:3) and through righteousness (Proverbs 15:6). In fact, Proverbs 3:33 is even more specific: "The Lord's curse is on the house of the wicked, but he blesses the dwelling of the righteous."

More importantly, home is a foretaste of the eternal haven that awaits us when Jesus returns. He did not leave us to prepare another cubicle in His Father's office—thank God! It is not a competitive and impersonal meritocracy that inhabits heaven. It is the refuge of home—with a place in it for each of us—that Jesus promised. "Let not your hearts be troubled. Believe in God; believe also in me. In my Father's house are many rooms. If it were not so, would I have told you that I go to prepare a place for you? And if I go and prepare a place for you, I will come again and will take you to myself, that where I am you may be also" (John 14:1–3).

"Just a housewife" is a phrase our culture uses to undermine the importance of the private sphere. Though the marketplace does not value the home beyond what goods can be purchased for it, the ministry to be found there is of immense worth to the Lord. The stability of family relationships, the care of elderly or disabled family members, the discipling and training of children, the warm reception of guests, the making of a lifetime of memories, the daily modeling of biblical instruction, the fresh nourishment in an age of processed foods that contribute to our general ill health, the joy of a Christ-centered marriage—all of these things have long-lasting, if not eternal, effects. But most have little to no value in the marketplace. If we are wise, we will recognize this fact and consider whether the choices we are making are either actively building up or tearing down our homes (Proverbs 14:1 NIV)—for Scripture gives us no middle ground here.

DENTS IN THE DRYER

YEARS AGO, I HEARD SOMEONE TALKING about the need for margin in our lives—the built-in "breathing space" to absorb emergencies and unexpected delays in our schedules. From my observation, margin seems to disappear for working mothers. That's one of the reasons for the undercurrent of stress, low-grade guilt, and even anger that plagues these multitasking wives and mothers. I understand that many women enjoy working and others have to work, but here's a story that challenges feminism's perspective on the home and the contributions women make there. I don't offer it to say this is what every woman should do, nor that women should not have professional skills. Please note that my friend Megan did not drop out of her field—she just scaled back to doing occasional contract work from home. But her priorities shifted, and the results for everyone concerned were more profound than she would have guessed initially.

The electrical fire was the last straw. After the fire department left, Megan stood in the scorched remains of her laundry room, looked at the smoke and water damage, and vented all her frustration in one gutteral scream.

"I can't TAKE this anymore!"

The children began crying from the next room, frightened by their mother's anger.

Megan kicked the dryer three times, leaving a dent. "This is the last straw!" she yelled. "Can anything else go wrong? I can't handle all these *problems!*"

Her husband's face appeared in the doorway. "Are you insane? Stop it! Don't break anything else."

Megan looked at Peter, momentarily tempted to kick him too. Then the adrenaline left her and she backed down from a fight.

"Yeah, you're right. But I am seriously *stressed!* Why is it that something major always happens around here when I'm on deadline? I have to get those financials done tonight. My entire day was blown with meetings. Can you clean up here?"

Peter's face tightened. "I guess you've forgotten my article is due tomorrow morning."

Megan started to say something biting, but clamped her mouth shut in-stead. The house smelled acrid, the clothes—clean and dirty alike—that had been collected in the laundry room were beyond hope for wearing again, no doubt one of the kids needed homework help, and they were both on deadline.

"Well, I am obviously not superwoman," she finally said. "It's taken me to hit the big 4-0 to give up that illusion. I can't have it all. I can't do it all. And I'm not enjoying any of it. I am just an angry, tired woman with a to-do list three miles long."

She smiled a tight smile, trying to make light of her complaint.

Peter sighed. "Then let's stop trying. I'm sick of the to-do list. And I miss my fun wife."

"What are you saying?"

"Let's just live simply. Listen, the boys need more of our attention now. And, um, so does this house. Why are we making ourselves crazy? Let's stop doing so much. Let's try to live on one income. At least let's think about it, okay?"

Peter reached for his wife's hand. "And let's leave this stinky room."

It took a few months, but that wild-hair idea took root. Megan arranged to do contract work from home and then gave notice to her company. When they told the kids that she was quitting full-time work, the boys actually jumped up and down with excitement. Megan was a little surprised by their enthusiasm.

At first, she wondered how she would fill her days. She quickly made a schedule, assigning ongoing household tasks to different days. She thought she'd have a lot of time for scrapbooking or other neglected hobbies, but soon she saw that the care and feeding of four people could be quite time-consuming. Now that she was home, there was time to do the important things that never squeaked quite as loudly as the urgent things—making meals for sick neighbors, hosting a Bible study, visiting one of the elderly women from her church. She even had time to be a fun wife again. No longer did date night have to consist of running to Home Depot to get an item for whatever needed repair. In fact, she found she quite enjoyed having her weekends back again—no more Saturday errands with two little bodies strapped down in car seats all day.

One day her five-year-old skipped into the room and wrapped his arms around her waist. "Mommy, I love you now."

"Now?" Megan replied, smiling.

"Yeah, now. I love you now because you're much happier, and that makes me happier." He squeezed her waist really hard and then ran back down to the basement.

Megan burst into tears, a mixture of guilt and happiness. The kids were so young; she didn't think they had noticed.

A few years later, Megan had the opportunity to give her testimony to the newly married couples Sunday school class. In it, she challenged the young couples to renew their thinking about the home from the Bible's perspective:

> You know, I grew up thinking that homemaking wasn't that big a deal. I didn't like housework, so I thought I could get around it by hiring out for everything. At one point, I had a maid and a personal chef. I was too busy to clean or cook. And that sort of worked for a while. It took a lot of juggling, but in my mind it was worth it.
>
> But once the stress level got to be too much, I really had to carefully consider my decisions. Was I living the life God outlined for me in His Word? I took time to find out the importance of homemaking from a biblical perspective. And I found making a home is not about all your stuff or even doing household chores. It's more than just how you take care of your personal space. It's what Titus 2 talks about—how you fulfill your role in the church and in your relationships with other people, and how you glean from them and disciple others. Just to stay home, isolate yourself, and have a nicely decorated, tidy house is not the point. I can understand why people would be critical of that.
>
> Being at home involves all the practical management—grocery shopping, budgeting, getting the gutters clean, making sure the furnace is serviced. I also make sure everybody is going to the doctor, has the right medicine, that everybody eats and has clean clothes. But it also involves extending hospitality, caring for neighbors, babysitting others' children, making meals for someone, hosting people from other churches and other countries. It's always about the people. Making a home is not about the physical space; it's about the people who are coming and going from this place.
>
> But I'll be honest. There are times I miss working. There are two things I miss specifically. One: you can go out for lunch or coffee just

because you want a break. And two: it's easy to talk to other people—lengthy, uninterrupted conversations! One day, I may return to my career, but for now I wouldn't trade our more peaceful family schedule for anything!

And, really, it's not just you and your husband. It's never going to be just you and your husband. There are always other people. You want to bless your husband and make him your priority, but he is not the sole object of your life. That's foolish and it robs you from the blessings that come from sowing into God's purposes for the body of Christ. We have to remember that God has a call on our lives and His business is *always* about people.

Now whenever Megan does the laundry, she often looks at the dent in her dryer and whispers a prayer of thanksgiving to God. Make no mistake—the laundry *always* had to get done. But now she has time to enjoy her family too. And that is invaluable.

Six

THE
Mommy Wars

*T*his is a chapter that childless women or women with grown children may be tempted to skip. Don't do it! At this writing, I'm also a childless woman, but this is my favorite chapter in the book and the one about which I am most passionate. Chances are, you carry some ideas about children, contraception, and motherhood that have their roots in feminism. We've all been affected by this movement—it's hard to avoid. Motherhood has absorbed some hard blows in the previous centuries, but children have been hit harder. If you didn't know that the founder of the birth control movement identified with the eugenics movement of Nazi Germany, or that there are an estimated 100 million missing girls in this world, or that your fertility window is more limited than what the media portrays, read on. The real mommy wars are much bigger than you might expect!

⸻

"THERE IS SOMETHING ABOUT the phrase, 'Mommy Wars,' that makes me want to gouge out my own eyeballs with a fork, rather than have to read it ever again," wrote one blogger after reading yet another controversial article on the topic.[1]

Twenty years of media hype would undoubtedly elicit that reaction. The term was coined in the late 1980s by *Child* magazine to describe the tension that existed between working and stay-at-home mothers.[2] Since then, numerous books and articles have been published about the so-called mommy wars, feeding the talk show circuit and fueling blogosphere brushfires.

Why is this such an enduring topic? It's because of our nation's long-standing conflicted attitude toward the importance and function of mothers. Journalist Ann Crittenden captured the bittersweet reaction women often experience when they add the role of mother to the various identities they had before children. In her introduction to *The Price of Motherhood: Why the Most Important Job in the World Is Still the Least Valued*, Crittenden writes:

> Being a good-enough mother, I found, took more patience and inner strength—not to mention intelligence, skill, wisdom, and love—than my previous life had ever demanded. Nurturing and guiding an ever-changing child was not like housework, a checklist of domestic chores, but highly skilled labor, informed by the same spirit that inspires the best teachers, ministers, counselors, and therapists.
>
> The second surprise came when I realized how little my former world seemed to understand, or care, about the complex reality I was discovering. The dominant culture of which I had been a part considered child-rearing unskilled labor, if it considered child-rearing at all. And no one was stating the obvious: if human abilities are the ultimate fount of economic progress, as many economists now agree, and if those abilities are nurtured (or stunted) in the early years, then mothers and other caregivers of the young are the most important producers in the economy. They do have, literally, the most important job in the world.
>
> I'll never forget the moment I realized that almost no one else agreed. It was at a Washington, D.C., cocktail party, when someone asked, "What do you do?" I replied that I was a new mother, and they promptly vanished. I was the same person this stranger might have found worthwhile had I said I was a foreign correspondent for *Newsweek*, a financial reporter for the *New York Times*, or a Pulitzer prize nominee, all of which had been true. But as a mother, I had shed status like the skin off a snake.

I gradually realized that mothers—and everyone else who spends much time with children—were still in the same boat that women had been in only a few years earlier. After fighting hard to win respect in the workplace, women had yet to win respect for their work at home.

But the moment of truth came a few years after I had resigned from the *New York Times*, in order to have more time for my infant son. I ran into someone who asked, "Didn't you used to be Ann Crittenden?"

That's when I knew I had to write this book.[3]

I laughed when I read this wry scenario because it has as much to do with the self-promoting and cynical cultures of cities such as New York and Washington, D.C., as it does with any estimation of motherhood. But Crittenden hits a nerve with this illustration.

I would agree: Motherhood has taken a severe blow in terms of respect. But children have actually taken a greater blow, as I will discuss later in this chapter. And neither is a contemporary phenomenon. As we saw in the previous chapter, culturally, the roots of the "mommy wars" go back almost two hundred years.

But *spiritually*, the war goes back to the very first mother, Eve. Her assignment, along with her husband, Adam, was to be "fruitful and multiply and fill the earth" (Genesis 1:28). So when the Lord God cursed the Serpent that deceived her, He showed how the battle would be fought against this command to be fruitful and multiply. "And I will put enmity between you and the woman, and between your offspring and hers; he will crush your head, and you will strike his heel" (Genesis 3:15 NIV).

Ever since, Satan has labored to destroy the offspring of those who are made in the image of God. *The real mommy wars are not against flesh and blood—other mothers and their parenting methods—but against the one who seeks to destroy the next generation of those who would rise up to praise God.* We can debate all kinds of parenting philosophies, methods, and practices, but the real conflict is not with the proponents of opposite ideas. Most assuredly, there *is* a war and the price is high. Mothers (and fathers) are called to be strong warriors in this battle. But, as we've explored before in this book, Ephesians 6:12 tells us that our true opponents are not flesh and blood but the spiritual forces of evil in this present darkness.

And in this battle, the casualties are numerous.

Let's explore why.

The Mommy Tax

As I mentioned in the previous chapter, the issues of domesticity and child rearing are often interlinked. When feminist author and lawyer Linda Hirshman claimed women were making a huge mistake if they left full-time jobs to stay at home and care for their children, she bolstered her argument with the following analysis:

> Bad deals come in two forms: economics and home economics. The economic temptation is to assign the cost of child care to the woman's income. If a woman making $50,000 per year whose husband makes $100,000 decides to have a baby, and the cost of a full-time nanny is $30,000, the couple reason that, after paying 40 percent in taxes, she makes $30,000, just enough to pay the nanny. So she might as well stay home. This totally ignores that both adults are in the enterprise together and the demonstrable future loss of income, power, and security for the woman who quits. Instead, calculate that all parents make a total of $150,000 and take home $90,000. After paying a full-time nanny, they have $60,000 left to live on.[4]

What's missing from her analysis is the additional stress on the family from two people juggling careers and overseeing their various vendors (nanny, cleaning service, dog walker, etc.), while still trying to parent their children. Additionally, she falls into the same mind-set about the economics of child care that Ann Crittenden discusses in *The Price of Motherhood*—no matter how you put a price tag on it, mothers—and their substitutes—are severely undervalued in any economic discussion. In Hirshman's illustration, the presumably female nanny is only worth a portion of the wages the other adults are commanding.

Now Crittenden, who is a feminist, does not fall into traditional feminist thinking that success in work and life should emulate a masculine model. In fact, she is deeply disappointed that mainstream feminist organizations still devalue motherhood and a woman's role in the family. "What is needed is across-the-board recognition—in the work-place, in the family, in the law, and in social policy—that someone has to do the necessary work of raising children and sustaining families, and that the reward for such vital work should not be professional marginalization, a loss of status, and an increased risk of poverty," she writes.[5] This cluster of problems and the resulting lifetime loss of income is what she terms the "mommy tax"—a tax that she, like many mothers, has been more than willing to pay when she considers her own children. But she still maintains it is bad policy.

The Unproductive Housewife

Crittenden says the origins of the "mommy tax" can be traced back to the nineteenth century and the invention of the "unproductive housewife":

> As the story of the family is conventionally told, virtually all serious economic activity had left the household by mid-nineteenth century, as manufacturing migrated from farms into factories. The household evolved from a work-place, where most necessities were produced, into a place of leisure, consumption, and emotional replenishment; a "haven in a heartless world." Ostensibly, industrialization put families, and the women in them, "out of business."
>
> In fact, the family remained an intrinsic part of the economy. There was simply a transformation of the type of goods and services produced in the home. The new domestic product was the intensively raised child. According to anthropologist Wanda Minge-Klevana: "During the transition from preindustrial society to industrial society, the family underwent a qualitative change as a labor unit—from one that produced food to one whose primary function was to socialize and educate laborers for an industrial labor market."[6]

Here we have Republican Motherhood, remember? But for all of its earnest intentions, this doctrine of separate spheres became the underlying reason for why housewives and mothers suddenly dropped out of the economic valuation. In the new economy, work solely mattered if you could put a price on it. But the only way men could be successful in the industrial marketplace was if they could delegate the family and household functions to their wives. So successful husbands and intensively raised children became the valuable product of the unpaid work of married women—women who were still hindered by the lowly legal status of wives under coverture. (In its strictest sense, coverture meant a wife could not engage in suits or contracts, have her own assets, or execute legal documents without her husband's collaboration. Nor was she responsible for herself in legal or civil matters—her husband was. He was the full political and legal representative for her.[7]) Therefore, in evaluating the economic worth of women, the earliest first-wave feminists pushed for a literal, legal interpretation of the doctrine of separate spheres. Crittenden summarizes their thinking this way: "If women's work in the home is so exalted, they asked, why isn't it valued equally with men's work? By virtue of their labor, they argued, wives earned joint rights to all the property accumulated during marriage."[8]

This argument might have worked, but two events conspired to kill that idea and to push the definition toward the "unproductive housewife." The first was that in 1870—the same year that the Fifteenth Amendment was ratified, granting black men, but not women, the right to vote—the U.S. economy reached a significant milestone. For the first time in American history, more men were earning wages than were producing their own livelihoods. As Crittenden writes, in this new cash economy, the principal economic unit was no longer the household but the individual, a change that was reflected in the way the U.S. Census gathered data. Previously, the federal census had measured economic activity by the number of *families* engaged in a particular enterprise. But by the 1860 census, the profession, occupation, or trade of each *individual* over the age of fifteen was noted.

With this kind of wage-based classification system, it took a mere forty years more for the census to officially classify wives/mothers and daughters without paying jobs as "dependents."[9]

The first blow in the modern mommy wars was struck.

The second blow came in the form of social Darwinism. In her 1898 book *Women and Economics: A Study of the Economic Relation between Men and Women as a Factor in Social Evolution*, feminist Charlotte Perkins Gilman said "the salient fact in this discussion is that, whatever the economic value of the domestic industry of women is, they do not get it."[10] Thus, Gilman attempted to remedy this situation by applying Darwinism-influenced business and scientific principles to the home and child rearing. Claiming that women would need "thousands of years and several generations to adapt" to the economic independence of men, and that "the lines of social relation today are mainly industrial," Gilman suggested many reforms, including the premise that child rearing should become professionalized as a collective activity: "All human life in its very nature is open to improvement, and motherhood is not excepted."[11]

In her writing and speaking, Gilman maintained that the vast majority of American women were not only unproductive but also indolent. "It is the female of our race, who holds a parasitic place, dependent on the male," she wrote.[12] Her solution was to collectivize domestic labor and "break up that relic of the patriarchal age—the family as an economic unit." Gilman would dismantle the private home and replace it with apartment houses with professionally staffed facilities for meals, cleaning, laundry, and child care.[13] She concluded that "women would never undergo evolutionary progress as long as they remained isolated in the pre-scientific environment of the home."[14]

Gilman constructed her own life as close as possible to her theories. In 1884, she married an artist named Charles Walter Stetson, and she gave birth to their only child, Katharine Beecher Stetson, a year later. Four years after they married, Gilman separated from her husband; they were divorced in 1894. That same year, she sent Katharine to live with her ex-husband and his second wife, a woman who was one of her closest friends. In her memoir, she wrote that she was happy to do this because Katharine's second mother was "fully[as] good as the first."[15]

As Crittenden explains, Gilman represented the future direction of the women's movement:

> [A]t the turn of the twentieth century, the women's movement contained two contradictory strands: one that denigrated women's role within the family, and one that demanded recognition and remuneration for it. The first argued that only one road could lead to female emancipation, and it pointed straight out of the house toward the

world of paid work. The second sought equality for women within the family as well and challenged the idea that a wife and mother was inevitably an economic "dependent" of her husband.

For the rest of the twentieth century, the women's movement followed the first path, and it led to innumerable great victories. But in choosing that path, many women's advocates accepted the continued devaluation of motherhood, thereby guaranteeing that feminism would not resonate with millions of wives and mothers.[16]

Crittenden is generous in her assessment of "numerous great victories" for women. But she correctly assesses the path of the modern women's movement.

"The Clogs and Destroyers of Civilization"

With motherhood so devalued by the close of the nineteenth century, it's not surprising that children became the target of twentieth-century activists. What may surprise many people is to know that the charge was led single-handedly by a woman, herself a mother of three. It is the third—and most serious—blow in the mommy wars.

Margaret Sanger was the founder of the modern birth control movement and a vocal proponent of eugenics—the theory of race improvement that was the cornerstone of Nazi Germany. Sanger believed that all evils stemmed from large families, especially large families of those she deemed as unfit. As she wrote in her 1920 book *Woman and the New Race*, "The most merciful thing that a large family does to one of its infant members is to kill it."[17]

I can't even fathom saying such a thing, but Sanger's personal history undoubtedly influenced her thinking. She was born in 1879 in Corning, New York, the sixth of eleven surviving children. Her father was a stonemason and a supporter of radical socialist causes. Sanger's mother succumbed to tuberculosis at forty-nine. Sanger later said the strain of eighteen pregnancies was what broke her mother's health.[18]

Sanger went on to study nursing and married in 1902. Her first pregnancy was a difficult one that landed her in a sanitarium for her confinement and recovery. But she regained her health and gave birth to two more children. In 1910, she began to work as a midwife and home nurse on the Lower East Side of New York City. A year later, she joined a radical labor movement and participated in several labor strikes.

By 1912, Sanger began writing a series of articles on female sexuality and contraception in the socialist publication *The Call*, in bold defiance of then-current laws against the dissemination of information on sexually transmitted diseases and contraception. Two years later, by then separated from her husband whom she would later divorce, she founded the monthly magazine *Woman Rebel*, under the slogan, "No gods; no masters!"[19] In 1914, she fled to Europe after she was indicted for violating U.S. postal obscenity laws. But two years later, having avoided imprisonment, she was back in the United States to open the nation's first birth control clinic, in Brooklyn, New York. After ten days of operation, she was arrested and jailed. The trial made her a national figure, and it handed doctors the right to prescribe birth control advice.

In 1921, Sanger organized the American Birth Control League, which later became the Planned Parenthood Federation of America. For Sanger, the birth control movement was founded on two goals: limiting the reproduction of the "unfit" and challenging Christian teaching by creating a "new morality." She campaigned against women "with staggering rapidity" breeding "those numberless, undesired children who become the clogs and the destroyers of civilization."[20] Sanger's scorched-earth writing left no one guessing about her views:

> While unknowingly laying the foundations of tyrannies and providing the human tinder for racial conflagrations, woman was also unknowingly creating slums, filling asylums with insane, and institutions with other defectives. She was replenishing the ranks of the prostitutes, furnishing grist for the criminal courts and inmates for prisons. Had she planned deliberately to achieve this tragic total of human waste and misery, she could hardly have done it more effectively.[21]
>
> [T]he most urgent problem to-day is how to limit and discourage the over-fertility of the mentally and physically defective. Possibly drastic and Spartan methods may be forced upon American society if it continues complacently to encourage the chance and chaotic breeding that has resulted from our stupid, cruel sentimentalism.[22]

She was equally caustic about Christianity and the Bible's teaching on sexuality:

> Let it be realized that this creation of new sex ideals is a challenge to the church. Being a challenge to the church, it is also, in less degree, a challenge to the state. The woman who takes a fearless stand for the incoming sex ideals must expect to be assailed by reactionaries of every kind. Imperialists and exploiters will fight hardest in the open, but the ecclesiastic will fight longest in the dark. He understands the situation best of all; he knows what reaction he has to fear from the morals of women who have attained liberty. For, be it repeated, the church has always known and feared the spiritual potentialities of woman's freedom.[23]
>
> When women have raised the standards of sex ideals and purged the human mind of its unclean conception of sex, the fountain of the race will have been cleansed. Mothers will bring forth, in purity and in joy, a race that is morally and spiritually free.[24]

I think it's safe to say that with the perspective of nearly a century of hindsight, we have hardly attained a cleansed human race that is morally and spiritually free. To expect this kind of salvation from women is unwise, unbiblical, and downright impossible. As we will see in a following chapter, women did *not* manage to raise the sex standard—in fact, third-wave feminism gave rise to the feminine "raunch culture" we live in today. Yet Sanger was so confident about the fruits of birth control and the new race that she predicted exactly the *opposite* of what has come to pass:

> When motherhood becomes the fruit of a deep yearning, not the result of ignorance or accident, its children will become the foundation of a new race. There will be no killing of babies in the womb by abortion, nor through neglect in foundling homes, nor will there be infanticide. . . .
>
> The relentless efforts of reactionary authority to suppress the message of birth control and of voluntary motherhood are futile. The powers of reaction cannot now prevent the feminine spirit from breaking its bonds. When the last fetter falls the evils that have resulted from the suppression of woman's will to freedom will pass. Child slavery,

prostitution, feeblemindedness, physical deterioration, hunger, oppression and war will disappear from the earth. . . . When the womb becomes fruitful through the desire of an aspiring love, another Newton will come forth to unlock further the secrets of the earth and the stars. There will come a Plato who will be understood, a Socrates who will drink no hemlock, and *a Jesus who will not die upon the cross.* (emphasis added)[25]

God forbid. God *forbid*!

I type that quote with tears on my cheeks. Without the cross, we are doomed. There is no hope of new heavens and a new earth, free from the effects of the fall, without the atonement of our sinless Savior. There is no hope for mercy to triumph over judgment unless it be at the foot of that cross. There is no hope for "child slavery, prostitution, feeblemindedness, physical deterioration, hunger, oppression and war [to] disappear from the earth" if the Father's righteous anger against these terrible sins is not satisfied. Where would justice be in the universe if such sins go overlooked? No, on the contrary, our only hope *is* the cross! If Jesus had not been obedient to this plan of salvation, who could possibly be our mediator?

And who could possibly atone for the slaughter that eventually arose from this "new morality"? Only Jesus Christ, our Savior!

So let's not get lost in a smoke screen. I don't quibble with Sanger's observation that numerous pregnancies can be very hard on a woman's body or that poor families with many children can suffer tremendous financial hardship. *But right observation does not always lead to right interpretation.* Sanger saw poor health, poverty, sin, anger, abuse, and numerous other challenges and her interpretation was that the "unwanted" children were the root problem—or even that some people shouldn't reproduce at all. Thus, she was able to make the outrageous statement that "the most merciful thing that a large family does to one of its infant members is to kill it." That is the furthest thing from mercy! But her thinking has influenced our culture. Therefore, contraception is not the *true* issue of contention. (Abortifacients, however, are. We need to clearly distinguish between prevention and abortion.) Understanding Sanger helps us to understand why children are now disposable—seen as anything ranging from inconveniences to parasites—instead of being received as gifts from God.

Margaret Sanger lived to see the development of the first birth control pill in 1960—something she had worked toward. She died in 1966, the year the Johnson administration incorporated "family planning" into its foreign policy and domestic health and social welfare programs for the United States.[26] Her life bridged the first and second waves of feminism, but her philosophies were the booster rocket for the most profound effects of second-wave feminism.

Intrusion Confusion

Of the myriad changes created by second-wave feminism, the most pronounced would be the movement's unwavering commitment to abortion. This is where second-wave feminism parts most sharply with the first-wave, as nineteenth-century women's rights activists were generally pro-life. Elizabeth Cady Stanton, for example, called abortion infanticide and wrote, "When we consider that women are treated as property, it is degrading to women that we should treat our children as property to be disposed of as we see fit."[27]

Those who grew up in the shadow of *Roe v. Wade* may be surprised to find out that abortion was even a concern for Stanton and other nineteenth-century women. According to Marvin Olasky, author of *Abortion Rites*, abortion has been in America since at least 1629. Despite being illegal, abortion rates actually rose in the mid-nineteenth century to match—in terms of the proportion of population—the abortion rates of today. Olasky says three factors were responsible for this trend in the mid-1800s: the advent of the Industrial Revolution, the anonymity of the new cities that gave rise to prostitution, and the popularity of "a substantial nineteenth-century New Age movement (then called 'spiritism')." "One big difference between now and then is that most mid-nineteenth-century abortions occurred among prostitutes, who probably averaged four per year," Olasky writes.[28] He agrees with another historian who says the medicines and procedures used for these abortions may have been a primary cause for their shortened life spans.[29]

This spiritism movement, which peaked around 1860, anticipated the free love movement of the late 1960s by more than a century.

Based on the belief that the living can and do communicate with the spirits of the departed through séances and mediums, spiritism also anticipated the "question authority" motto of the 1960s and 1970s. Thus, practitioners rejected the conventions of the day, including monogamy and motherhood.

According to B. F. Hatch, a doctor who wrote about spiritism in 1859, "women who have abandoned their husbands . . . and who are living in adultery with their paramours, produce abortion, and arise from their guilty couches and stand before large audiences as the medium for angels." He wrote that the spiritists of that time "boastingly speak of their freedom from what they call social conventionalism and the superstitions of Christianity." Having once been prominent in this movement until he began to witness its results, Hatch wrote of the intensely self-centered beliefs of the movement, saying that spiritists "earnestly contend that no external authority, and no code of human laws can justly bind their affections, or interfere with their liberty to follow the impulse of their personal affinities."[30] One Vermont meeting of spiritists passed in 1858 a set of resolutions that claimed "the authority of each individual soul is absolute and final, in deciding questions as to what is true or false in principle, and right or wrong in practice"; and that "the most sacred and important right of woman is her right to decide for herself how often and under what circumstances she shall assume the responsibilities and be subject to the cares and sufferings of Maternity. . . ."[31]

Fast-forward a century, and you find the same thinking. Sanger's Planned Parenthood group was actively working in the 1950s and beyond to decriminalize abortion. Pro-abortion groups began to gain legal ground in the late 1960s and early 1970s. In 1969, Betty Friedan and Dr. Bernard Nathanson were among the founders of the National Association for Repeal of Abortion Laws (which later became the National Abortion Rights Action League and is now known as NARAL Pro-Choice America). By April 1970, one-fifth of U.S. states had approved measures allowing abortion, but in extreme conditions only. More liberal laws existed in New York, California, Hawaii, and Alaska. One article summarizes the history of *Roe v. Wade* this way:

In 1973, the U.S. Supreme Court handed down its *Roe v. Wade* decision. The woman at the center of the lawsuit, Norma McCorvey ("Jane Roe"), had challenged Texas' abortion law in 1969. At the time, she was pregnant and wanted an abortion—which was illegal. According to McCorvey, political opportunists grabbed hold of her case in an effort to further their pro-abortion agenda.

The court's decision in Roe's favor rested on two premises: a woman's "right to privacy," and the belief that the beginning of life cannot be pinpointed. Supreme Court Justice Harry Blackmun wrote the majority decision in *Roe v. Wade*, stating, "We need not resolve the difficult question of when life begins. When those trained in the respective disciplines of medicine, philosophy and theology are unable to arrive at any consensus, the judiciary, at this point in the development of man's knowledge, is not in a position to speculate as to the answer.[32]

Justice Blackmun's words were the mantra of the pro-abortion position at that time. However, with the commercial release of the ultrasound machine in 1976, that argument was no longer feasible. In fact, it led Dr. Bernard Nathanson, one of NARAL's founders and the former director of New York's largest abortion clinic, to recant his position in the late 1970s and become a vocal abortion opponent. Nathanson claims that he was responsible for more than 75,000 abortions in his career, including his own child. He is probably best known for the 1984 documentary *The Silent Scream*, which used ultrasound technology to reveal what happens during an abortion.

Because scientific advances have pushed Justice Blackmun's "difficult question of when life begins" to a reference point beyond the "viability" of the fetus, feminist activists only had a woman's "right to privacy" to promote pro-abortion thinking. "Keep your laws off my body" became a popular feminist slogan. From there, feminist ideology developed *bizarre* ideas, such as the 1996 argument advanced by Eileen McDonagh that we need to shift attention "from what the fertilized ovum 'is,' as it develops into a fetus and eventually into a baby, to what the fertilized ovum 'does,' as it causes pregnancy by implanting itself in a woman's body and maintaining that implantation for nine months." As she writes:

The fetus is the direct cause of pregnancy, and if it makes a woman pregnant without her consent, it severely violates her bodily integrity and liberty. Our culture, courts, and Congress have all ignored the fetus as the agent of pregnancy, with one telling exception: when the fetus threatens the woman's life. . . . Even in a medically normal pregnancy, the fetus massively intrudes on a woman's body and expropriates her liberty. If a woman does not consent to this transformation and use of her body, the fetus's imposition constitutes injuries sufficient to justify the use of deadly force to stop it. While it is not usual to think of pregnancy as an injury, that is exactly how the law already defines it when it is imposed on a woman without her consent. For example, when men or physicians expose women to the risk of pregnancy by means of rape or incompetent sterilization, and a pregnancy follows, the law clearly acknowledges that women have been seriously injured. This book expands the concept of wrongful pregnancy to include what the fertilized ovum does to a woman when it makes her pregnant without her consent. It is the only entity that can make a woman pregnant, and when it does so without her consent, it imposes the serious injuries of wrongful pregnancy even if the pregnancy in question is medically normal.[33]

The "logic" boggles the mind, doesn't it?! McDonagh writes as though the fertilized ovum is capable of independent action, and she misses the fact that women's (usually willing) sexual activity is what contributes to pregnancy.

Female Feticide

Even more appalling—in terms of women's rights—is that abortion is more dangerous for *female* fetuses than male fetuses. In fact, sex-selective abortions have cost *millions upon millions* of female lives. Couples in populous nations such as China and India routinely use ultrasound technology to determine if they are carrying a boy. Due to the strong cultural preference for a son, the female fetus is aborted. According to a 2007 report from the British medical journal *Lancet*, worldwide there are 100 million "missing girls" who should have been born but were not. Fifty million of them would have been Chinese and 43 million would have been Indian. The rest would have been born in Afghanistan, South Korea, Pakistan, and Nepal. In a 2007 series about the implications of sex selection and abortion, the *Washington Times* wrote:

> One Geneva-based research center, in a 2005 update on the phenomenon, termed it "the slaughter of Eve."
>
> "What we're seeing now is genocide," says Sabu George, a New Delhi-based activist. "We will soon exceed China in losing 1 million girls a year."
>
> The date may already be here. In a report released Dec. 12, UNICEF said India is "missing" 7,000 girls a day or 2.5 million a year.
>
> Although India has passed laws forbidding sex-specific abortions, legions of compliant doctors and lax government officials involved in India's $100 million sex-selection industry have made sure they are rarely enforced.
>
> Several companies, notably General Electric Corp., have profited hugely from India's love affair with the ultrasound machine.
>
> As a result, a new class of wifeless men are scouring eastern India, Bangladesh and Nepal for available women. India, already a world leader in sex trafficking, is absorbing a new trade in girls kidnapped or sold from their homes and shipped across the country.[34]

According to the *Washington Times*, "female feticide" is a $100 million industry in India. But there is evidence that the gospel is making some inroads there. The *Times* quotes one government official in Hyderabad, a city in south India, who noticed a religious divide in the sex ratios as reported in the 2001 national census. This official reported that Christians had the best sex ratios, and in highly Christianized areas, there were more women born than men.[35]

"My Daddy's Name Is Donor"

In 1915, Charlotte Perkins Gilman wrote the book *Herland*, a novel about a feminine utopia, a world populated by women who don't need men—not even to procreate. Motherhood is a central theme, but men are unnecessary for this function. Gilman, as we've seen earlier, is once again surprisingly prescient about the future. For not even a century later, a toddler wearing a T-shirt reading, "My daddy's name is Donor," made the national media. He was the son of a lesbian couple who wanted to "empower" their child by knocking down the shame of donor conception.

That viewpoint concerned author Elizabeth Marquardt, a researcher with the Institute for American Values, who later wrote a book about the ethical issues in reproductive technology. "What troubles me is that children today are being raised in an era of increasingly flexible definitions of parenthood, definitions that often serve the interests of adults without regard for children," she said. "We cannot assume that donor offspring easily forget about their biological parents just because the adults in their lives want them to. Banning donor anonymity is a good step, but it's not enough. Our culture needs a serious debate about the implications of technologies used to form many of today's alternative families, one that places the interests of the resulting children front and center."[36]

No doubt. The legal ramifications in an era of fluid families are immense. In a television show broadcast in 2000, Bernard Nathanson recounted a California legal case of Solomonic proportions:

> The problem in assisted reproductive technology is that it is turning upside down all of our relationships to each other. For example, there is egg donation and sperm donation, then surrogate mothers and embryo transplants and frozen embryos. The absurdity of this comes up in a case in California in which a trial judge had an eight-year-old girl appear before him. A couple who wanted a baby (the woman could not carry a child and the man had weak sperm) commissioned the assisted reproductive technologist to mix somebody else's sperm, the sperm donor, with somebody else's egg. They paid for it. They created an embryo, the embryo was put in the womb of a surrogate mother and she delivered the baby nine months later. Then the question arose as to who were the parents, and just about the time the question arose, the original couple who paid for all this filed for divorce. So the question became, was the original couple the parents of this child or was the sperm donor and his wife the parent or the egg donor and her husband the parent or the surrogate mother and her husband the parent? The judge concluded there were eight parents literally, biologically,

but the child had no parents and was placed in a foster home. I mean the permutations and combinations of this kind of technology are staggering.[37]

But what to do with the living child is just part of the story. For every successful child born through reproductive technology, there are several more frozen siblings—the embryos that were not implanted in that particular pregnancy. Some couples, unprepared for this moral dilemma, keep those embryos frozen indefinitely (paying the hefty storage fees). Others put their embryos up for adoption or donate them for scientific research. Some destroy the embryos. And a few have actually embroiled themselves in custody battles over the embryos.

The legal landscape is changing nearly daily on this issue as science gallops ahead of our culture's legal and ethical determinations on reproductive technology. I can only present a few issues here as they are beyond the scope of this book. They are not, however, outside the scope of the Bible, as we will soon examine.

That Biological Clock

For most young women, the greatest—and most subtle—impact of feminist ideology shows up in postponed fertility. Young women are groomed for career tracks, but not for motherhood. They believe that it is possible for women to "have it all." Those of us who have tried, however, know this is not true. It *may* be possible to have it all, but *not* at the same time. Even with reproductive technology, there are limits to the natural life of a woman's eggs. The choices women make as young adults may affect their ability to have children later on.

This is what author Sylvia Ann Hewlett inadvertently discovered as she set out in 1998 to do a study of the "breakthrough generation"—the women who crashed the career barriers to become successful in traditionally male occupations. While doing her interviews, Hewlett discovered that none of her subjects had children, and none had actually *chosen* to be childless. Childlessness was a result of their career dedication.

That discovery changed the subject of her book project; in 2002 she published *Creating a Life: Professional Women and the Quest for Children*. The book addressed the "creeping non-choice" of childlessness among successful women. One of the high-powered women Hewlett interviewed provided this sound piece of advice: "Ask yourself what you need to be happy at forty-five. And ask yourself this question early enough so that you have a shot of getting what you want. Learn to be as strategic with your personal life as you are with your career."[38]

In the "soft" feminism that's peddled every day in women's magazines, few write about the short window of optimum fertility in women's lives. According to the American Society of Reproductive Medicine (ASRM), "peak efficiency in the female reproductive system occurs in the early twenties with a steady decline thereafter."[39] And that's exactly when most young women are blithely unconcerned about marriage or motherhood.

As a result, in 2001 ASRM launched an ad campaign designed to raise awareness about the factors affecting women's fertility. The ads focused on four risks: smoking, sexually transmitted diseases, being overweight, and age, all of which affect women's ability to conceive. But only one risk factor—age—outraged the feminist group National Organization for Women (NOW). Despite feminist complaints about creating guilt trips with these ads, an ASRM spokesman explained "that the association wanted to run the ads because doctors were tired of having women in their late thirties and forties shocked, frustrated, and heartbroken to find that their dreams of having children had vanished."[40]

How prevalent is childlessness? According to U.S. Census Bureau data from a June 2002 survey, there are 26.7 million women ages fifteen to forty-four who are childless. "That's 44 percent of all the women in that age group—a record number, and 10 percent more than in 1990."[41] Some have chosen childlessness, if media reports are accurate, but many more women have inadvertently missed the opportunity to bear children by trying to imitate the life cycles of men. Fertility is a limited opportunity for women and it should be cherished.

There are millions of women who don't identify with the extreme views of radical feminism and would like to bear children—eventually. What they need to know is that if motherhood is important, it's important enough to plan for.

Put on the Full Armor of God

You may be a mother and in the thick of rearing children right now. Perhaps it took you many weeks to read this chapter, thanks to the constant interruptions of young children. Your daily life may consist of dozens of repetitive tasks that feel so mundane and irrelevant. You kiss boo-boos, you make dinner, you do dishes, you answer a homework question, you drive to soccer practice, you read a good-night story, you do laundry, you make dinner again. Unglamorous daily tasks and unimportant in the big picture, you may think.

This is absolutely not true! *You are engaged in spiritual warfare*, battling against beliefs and philosophies that slander God's name and tarnish His gifts to us. You are standing against those who believe heinous lies, like "the most merciful thing that a large family does to one of its infant members is to kill it." By giving life and nurturing life, you are reflecting the life-giving characteristics of our holy God! Made in His image, you are reflecting Him when you care for the lives He has created.

I think it is easy for mothers to lose sight of the big picture when they are consumed with the daily "ordinariness" of life. I hope that this chapter has helped you to see how relentless the assault against bearing and mothering children can be. I hope it has helped you to take the long view of what you are doing in training the next generation to be worshipers of God. None of us can make that happen—it is the regenerating work of the Holy Spirit in each of us—but we are called to plant and water the seeds of the gospel and wait with expectant hope that God will give the growth.

This applies to those of us who are childless too. Whether you are not yet married, or married but not yet pregnant, or single or widowed and past the age of bearing children—whatever season of life you are in, you are still part of the great community of believers, who are called to witness to the majesty of God: "One generation shall commend your works to another, and shall declare your mighty acts" (Psalm 145:4). It may be quite bitter right now not to have children of your own, but I ask you to consider how strategic you can be even now. Where can you stand against the Devil's schemes and invest in the children God has already put in your life? So many hurting children exist and so many are being discarded. In the mommy wars, every believing woman needs to enlist.

At the beginning of this chapter, I referenced the spiritual warfare theme of Ephesians 6:12. Let's consider that verse in the context of the surrounding passage.

> *Finally, be strong in the Lord and in his mighty power. Put on the full armor of God so that you can take your stand against the devil's schemes. For our struggle is not against flesh and blood, but against the rulers, against the authorities, against the powers of this dark world and against the spiritual forces of evil in the heavenly realms.* (Ephesians 6:10–12 NIV)

It bears repeating: Our true enemies are not the men and women named in this chapter, nor those who champion their thinking today. They oppose God and His people—that is true. They are pushing forward the Devil's schemes—*that* is true. We need to take a stand, but we need to heed how God tells us to do it. We are called to be strong *in the Lord*, not ourselves.

> *Therefore put on the full armor of God, so that when the day of evil comes, you may be able to stand your ground, and after you have done everything, to stand. Stand firm then, with the belt of truth buckled around your waist, with the breastplate of righteousness in place, and with your feet fitted with the readiness that comes from the gospel of peace. In addition to all this, take up the shield of faith, with which you can extinguish all the flaming arrows of the evil one. Take the helmet of salvation and the sword of the Spirit, which is the word of God. And pray in the Spirit on all occasions with all kinds of prayers and requests. With this in mind, be alert and always keep on praying for all the saints.* (Ephesians 6:13–18 NIV)

Twice in this passage we are told to put on God's protective armor. God's armor is not the self-protective effort we make to preserve our reputation, our pride, and our flesh. Our armor begins with knowing His truth and living with it fastened around us. It is found in protecting our hearts, the wellspring of life, with the righteousness that comes from Christ's finished work on the cross. It is living prepared to share the gospel of peace—in words and in deeds—at all times.

Most importantly, it means lifting up that shield of faith—the confessions of our mouth and the thoughts of our hearts—against the fiery darts from the Father of Lies. It means going to battle equipped with an accurate knowledge of the Scriptures. And it means *constant* prayer. These are not flippant or quick tasks. They require purposeful investment in the spiritual disciplines in order to be well-armed, ready for the battle.

Biblical Esteem

The history of feminist ideology is manifestly anti-mother, anti-child, and anti-Jesus. What's less clear is how much each of us has been affected, or even infected, by this agenda. It's good to know, for example, the worldview behind the tools we take for granted, such as contraception. Which of these tools can be received with gratitude and used with thanksgiving is an issue of Christian liberty and wisdom, tempered with faith toward God. But we should be suspicious of how much we have been influenced by our culture. For example, are children a blessing and a gift, as the Bible says, or an inconvenience or even unwanted intrusion? The Bible says it is God who opens the womb, so are we willing to receive a child at any time as a gift from His hand?

The Bible clearly esteems children; even Jesus gave children special favor. He healed them, He welcomed them, He encouraged His disciples to emulate childlike trust and faith. As Andreas Köstenberger writes in *God, Marriage, and Family:*

> Jesus did not deal with children merely on the level of what they should do or think but on the level of who they were in God's eyes. Studying how Jesus understood children can help us know how we should view and relate to our own and other children. Jesus' earthly ministry intersected with children on a number of occasions. As mentioned, Jesus more than once *restored children to their parents by way of miraculous healing.* In one instance, Jesus put a child in the disciples' midst as an example of the nature of discipleship, asserting that, "Whoever received one such child in my name receives me, and whoever receives me, receives not me but him who sent me" (Mark 9:36–37 and parallels). This

must have been startling for Jesus' audience, since in his day it would have been uncommon for adults to think they could learn anything from a child.

The climactic pronouncement, "I tell you the truth, anyone who will not receive the kingdom of God like a little child will never enter it" (Mark 10:15 NIV), ties together the earlier-recorded instances of Jesus' receptivity toward children with an important characteristic of the kingdom, a humble lack of regard for one's own supposed status. . . . For Jesus, there is no better way to illustrate God's free, unmerited grace than pointing to a child.[42]

The Bible is also clearly "pro-life" in the sense of cherishing and protecting life. Whenever children were used by ancient cultures to promote their self-seeking idolatry, God thundered against it. He detested the wicked Ammorite practice of sacrificing children in a fire to appease the false god Molech (2 Kings 23:10), saying, "They built high places for Baal in the Valley of Ben Hinnom to sacrifice their sons and daughters to Molech, though I never commanded, nor did it enter my mind, that they should do such a detestable thing . . . " (Jeremiah 32:35 NIV).

The Scriptures present this "pro-life" stance as evidence of fearing God more than human rulers or powers. When the Hebrews were in Egypt and they became so numerous that the pharaoh was concerned they would become too mighty and fight against them, he ordered the slaughter of Hebrew male babies in a vain attempt to control them.

Then the king of Egypt said to the Hebrew midwives, one of whom was named Shiphrah and the other Puah, "When you serve as midwife to the Hebrew women and see them on the birthstool, if it is a son, you shall kill him, but if it is a daughter, she shall live." But the midwives feared God and did not do as the king of Egypt commanded them, but let the male children live. So the king of Egypt called the midwives and said to them, "Why have you done this, and let the male children live?" The midwives said to Pharaoh, "Because the Hebrew women are not like the Egyptian women, for they are vigorous and give birth before the midwife comes to them." So God dealt well with the midwives. And the people multiplied and grew very strong. And because the midwives feared God, he gave them families. (Exodus 1:15–21, emphasis added)

These women would not obey one of the most powerful rulers on earth because they honored God more than human opinion or might. They would not murder innocent children, and as a result, the Lord gave them children of their own to cherish and nurture. They were willing to stand up to the evil attack against the next generation.

On the days when you experience what Ann Crittenden experienced—that as a mother you "shed status like a skin off a snake"—remember that your role is important to God. The command to honor your father *and mother* is enshrined in the Ten Commandments (Deuteronomy 5:16) and is the only one to come with a promise of blessing. And Proverbs celebrates the teaching and wisdom of both a father and a mother.

Finally, I make a plea to those whose children are grown and on their own. Our culture says you are "empty nesters." I much prefer the term a friend coined, "open nesters." Your nest is now open to minister to a variety of people. You also have a strategic place in the war against mothers and children. Your assignment comes from Titus 2:3–5: "Older women likewise are to be reverent in behavior, not slanderers or slaves to much wine. They are to teach what is good, and *so train the young women to love their husbands and children*, to be self-controlled, pure, working at home, kind, and submissive to their own husbands, *that the word of God may not be reviled*" (emphasis added).

Feminism seeks to revile God's name and Word. It has sown much discord and false teaching, and young women today are reaping the bad fruit. In fact, many are reaping as sleepwalkers. They aren't even aware of what they are doing and thinking—it just seems like second nature. They need the life perspective of older women—they need your testimonies of God's faithfulness, numerous praise reports from the years you have walked with God. Younger women need your instruction in both the practical and spiritual aspects of motherhood. In fact, the need is so great that the marketplace is stepping in to meet it, having sniffed out the opportunity for a profit. When Titus 2 mentors aren't available, mothers have no choice but to turn to commercial consultants, paying $250 for an initial meeting with a potty-training coach and $175 per follow-up visit or $250 to $500 per consultation for a sleep trainer.[43] Your counsel is obviously valuable for practical matters. How much more so in terms of spiritual matters for mothers and children?

The "mommy wars" are real. And they are more significant and more costly than most of us ever contemplate. May we not be discouraged or diminished by the opinion of our culture, so that we can keep our eyes on the high calling of motherhood found in the Bible.

MATERNAL GRACE

I LOVE TO COLLECT THE TALES of the Lord's faithfulness. I think we all need to hear various accounts of how God has answered prayers, but I carry a soft spot in my heart for women who are making the long-term investment in another human being. We covered a lot of sobering material in the mommy wars chapter. To offer an encouraging perspective, here are the stories of several women who have had profound encounters with God in conceiving, bearing, rearing, and adopting children. This is the longest collection of personal stories in the book because I hoped each of you would find some aspect of hope or help among these accounts. I know all of these women and their children—they are trophies of God's grace.

Pregnant Again

Elke is expecting her second child. As she talks about her past, she unconsciously strokes her belly, soothing the thirty-two-week-old baby within her.

"I'm having a boy," she says with a bright smile. "He's kicking a lot today."

She pauses, her smile fading. "I didn't really feel this with my first pregnancy."

Elke grew up in Belgium and came to the United States. almost ten years ago. She came for a short-term job, expecting to stay less than a year. But within a few months she had a new boyfriend . . . and no desire to leave. When he moved in with her, she began throwing up. Much to their surprise, Elke was pregnant—and having a rough go of it too. Despite the constant vomiting, she was excited about being pregnant and eager to keep her child. But her high hopes for the future didn't last long. Nauseated and exhausted, she didn't respond well when her boyfriend lost yet another job. So she kicked him out.

Maybe it was that "pregnancy glow" that led Elke to quickly start dating again. Her new boyfriend was a police officer in the process of a divorce. He already had one child and made it very clear that he didn't want any more children in the near future. Initially, Elke held her tongue about her pregnancy, fearful of losing him. But eventually, the course of nature forced her hand.

"It took awhile for me to tell my second boyfriend that I was pregnant," she recalls. "So when I told him, he was shocked. I wasn't about to lose him because of this baby, so I also told him I was wondering about keeping it. He encouraged an abortion—saying things like, 'Well, you're young and you need your freedom.'"

It was obvious to Elke that her boyfriend wasn't going to accept her child. In addition, the baby's father was black but her new boyfriend was white. "I was thinking, there's no way he was going to be happy with this baby because it would be obvious it wasn't his," Elke recalls. "My mind-set was definitely about how to stay as happy as possible. I saw my road to happiness and this was in the way of it. It needed to move so that I could stay happy. Even giving up the baby—that was never an option. That would involve too much personal embarrassment and too many questions. It was too much work for me to go through. Abortion was the easy, quick fix."

So Elke sought the advice of a woman at work who was open about her three abortions.

The first thing she learned was that she was too far along for an abortion in her home state. She would have to go to a city in a nearby state to have an abortion because she was in her second trimester. Because she was so advanced, it was also going to be more expensive—around $3,000. So she called her mother to borrow the money, lying to her that there was something wrong with the baby so she had to abort it.

"I think the hardest thing for me about the abortion—besides the fact I had one—is the way it happened. It haunts me at times," she says, crying at the memory. "It was a two-day process. I had to go in a day early so that they could insert something in my cervix to dilate it. So I had a day to think about it, but my mind was already made up. I didn't consider changing my mind after I got the referral. I also don't remember anybody ever asking me about alternatives. They gave me some kind of pills beforehand and the doctor had told me I would have some pain. I didn't ask a lot of questions. I didn't want to know.

"I was getting cramps before I came in for the procedure. During the procedure, I was given some kind of IV medication. It was very bright in there, and the nurse kept me busy by asking me about my favorite vacation or positive memories. She was trying to distract me from what was going on and trying to make it a positive memory. There was a constant jerking and motion going on. There were times when the doctor would take a tool and go in and do something—which meant either severing a limb or breaking something because it wouldn't fit into the suction hose. But I knew that the skull wasn't going to be as small as that hose—they had to crush the skull before extracting the baby. It's so gruesome; it's just so awful. And it is *very* painful. Looking back on it, it is a butcher's work. But I wanted him to do it. I can't say I blame the doctor.

"Afterward, I was very crampy and bleeding a lot. They told me to have someone stay with me the first night because I could run a fever. I had a few more days of bed rest and took antibiotics for five days. You almost think it's going to be something simple, like a Pap smear. It takes a lot longer than you think it would, and there's no emotion involved on the part of anyone involved. So afterward it's common to have a real emotional backlash. I threw myself into work, just so I didn't have time to think. I didn't want to consider whether this was a real person or just an egg. I had this growing sense that I had done something wrong, but I didn't want to think about it. I think you can have a real experience of the consequences of your sin, even if you don't know anything about sin—because this is what happened to me."

Ashamed of her abortion, Elke told people she simply "lost" the baby. Her boyfriend brought her food and took care of her for the first two days, but soon distanced himself. There was a crime crisis going on and his police unit was on call a lot. But even after that resolved, he was harder and harder to reach. They eventually drifted apart.

At the same time, a Christian man at work began to reach out to Elke and another coworker. He began a Bible study and invited them to participate. Then, after a few weeks, he offered to take them to church. Elke and her friend attended and ended up joining an evangelistically oriented small group. Week after week, she heard the truth about Jesus, sin, hell, salvation, the church, and much more in a relational atmosphere. By the end of this outreach course, Elke repented of her sins and put her trust in the saving work of Jesus Christ on the cross.

As a new Christian, she was eager to learn about Jesus and the Bible. In her studies, she became convinced that her abortion was sinful because it violated God's commandment not to murder. She also saw that God was the Creator of life and the One who provides for all His creatures. Even though she repented of her sin and selfishness before God, she still wrestled with condemnation and low-grade guilt. "Early on, in my small group, I remember really feeling condemned. I kept saying, 'But I've killed someone!' I felt I couldn't be under the same grace as the others. Then my group leader looked at me and said, 'You know, we've *all* killed someone.' And in that moment, it finally clicked: It was our sin, all of us, that sent Jesus to the cross—my sin . . . and everyone else's. And yet that was the very way I could be forgiven."

Six years later, she married a man she met in her church and became pregnant about a year later with their first child. She was in awe that God would be so kind to her after everything she had done.

"When I first got pregnant, one of my friends miscarried," Elke says. "I thought I deserved that—not her. She hadn't had an abortion. My husband had to help me understand I am now a new person in Christ. I'm not the same person who had an abortion. I've been forgiven of that sin. But for the first four months of the pregnancy, every step of the way, I kept thinking about how I had been here before."

Elke pauses, still rubbing her belly. "I can feel his rear end right here." She looks up, tears brimming in her eyes. "Life really is a miracle."

A Special Child

*C*heryl had waited a long time to get married and have children. She was over forty when she got pregnant the first time. Her first child was a boy, Josh. She got pregnant with her second, Billy, almost immediately. Her third wasn't planned.

"We had just moved into this house," Cheryl recalls, sitting one afternoon on her back deck. "I was forty-three and had two kids under two years old. When I did the pregnancy test, I was sure it was going to be negative. One of the kids was crying, so I put the test down and forgot about it for about thirty minutes while I was changing diapers. I was shocked when I came back and saw it was positive."

Cheryl's previous pregnancies had been difficult—full of morning sickness and other trials. She had delivered by C-section for both, so she was concerned about the impact on her body from the third pregnancy. But she recalls that her third was the easiest pregnancy of all.

"Everything was going very well up until I went to have my routine sonogram at five months. As I got in the car, I thought the Lord was saying to me,

'Today you will find out this child has Down syndrome.' I was all by myself; my husband couldn't go. So I was sort of prepared when the sonogram ended up taking such a long time. The technician said it was a girl, which was one thing that made me happy because my husband really wanted a girl. But then the technician didn't say much more, just scanning back and forth. Then she went out to get the doctor, saying it was routine. When the doctor came in, he, too, took a long time. He kept looking at her hands. Then he told me that she had three markers for Down syndrome."

The expectation from some seemed to be that, with this news, Cheryl would abort. But it was not an option that Cheryl and her husband, Paul, would consider. They did proceed with the amniocentesis and other prenatal tests, though, so that they could prepare properly for the baby's arrival.

"I wanted everyone to know everything they could about her before she was born, so that it would be peaceful in the delivery room and everyone needed on the medical staff would be present. We found out her heart was fine, her GI tract was fine, she had two arms and two legs, etc.," she recalls. "At that time, we were in a small church group where five of the six families—totally random—had handicapped children. All of them responded the same way: 'There will be challenges, but God will help you. It's not that big of a deal.' Meaning that your life won't fall apart, your marriage won't fall apart, you will find many blessings in unexpected places, and God will be there for you. The only people who were upset or concerned were those who didn't have handicapped children—which should have told me something.

"To his credit, Paul didn't flinch when he heard the results. He has such a confidence in the sovereignty of God that he pretty much took the news in stride and said, 'Okay, let's see what God has for us.' It was all about God for him, but in my case, unfortunately, it was all about me. When I found out about her, I thought things like, *What will other people think of me? How am I going to look? What if I'm old and have a Down syndrome child following me around, holding my hand? What are people going to say?* And then somebody actually said to me, 'I wouldn't mind having a Down syndrome child, but I wouldn't want to take him to a restaurant. People will stare.' Like, what in the world am I supposed to do with that opinion?"

Cheryl laughs freely at the memory and pauses to zip up her jacket as the early autumn chill sets in.

"While I was dealing with these thoughts—with several weeks to go before delivery—I drove down the road one day, and I felt the Lord say to me, 'If I sent you a genius, then you'd be someone really special, right?' I realized then that my biggest concern was about how people viewed me. To be honest, when I had my first two children, there were times when I thought, 'I've arrived. I have a wonderful husband. I have reproduced. I've gotten into the club!' So God was using this child to expose and shatter my self-glorifying concerns."

When Lori was born, the hospital staff went out of their way to make Cheryl feel like a queen, even giving her a private room. All of the nurses assigned to her had handicapped relatives too. One nurse was a Christian with a child who has a syndrome that affects how she looks on the outside, though mentally she is not at all impaired. That girl was thirteen at the time and, like every teen girl, was preoccupied with her appearance. She asked her mother why God made her this way.

"This nurse simply said to her daughter, the Bible says you are 'fearfully and wonderfully made' and that's what we know about this situation. That made me think, *Well, that Scripture doesn't offer any exceptions*," Cheryl says. "I've always tried to see Lori that way, and there's been much grace to do so. We can't imagine being without Lori—she's a part of us."

Lori is now seven years old, a cheerful girl who loves her brothers and is excited to play with them whenever she can. She relishes having dinner guests over and loves to set the table. She delights in fingernail polish. She is a big fan of girly-girl shoes and she can be quite particular about her clothes. And she's learned to dial the phone and eagerly request her friends to come over and play.

"Lori is teaching us to enjoy the moment and to be grateful for whatever is happening at the time. She is willing to work very hard to learn to write, to learn to read. The boys can complain about having to do more reading or more math, but she tries so hard because she wants to do well," Cheryl says. "She's a huge example to us."

Lori is currently enrolled in a speech class with some children who are a little older than she is. When she started, the older students teased her and made fun of her. The teacher warned Cheryl about it, so on the way home, Cheryl asked Lori what had happened. "Her answer was, 'I loved them.' What she meant was, 'They were mean to me but I tried to love them.' I was so blessed by that. She didn't say anything bad about them. Though she's not always able to articulate certain thoughts or comprehend certain ideas, she grasps what my husband means when he tells the children, 'You have to love people even when they can't love you back.'

"There's a quote I read somewhere—but I don't know who said it. The gist of it is that the gospel is so transcendent, the greatest minds in the world can spend their whole lives studying it and yet they may never fully comprehend it. But it's also so simple that my Down syndrome child can understand it and respond to it. The gospel can be a huge intellectual problem for some really smart people, but Lori gets it, she really does. She understands she's a sinner and that Jesus died for her sins, and that He's an ever-present help in times of trouble, and that she can do all things through Christ who strengthens her.

"And, really, what else do you need to know?" Cheryl says, laughing.

"It's Just What I Wanted"

Like Cheryl, Irene's third child was also a surprise. Her other children were already eight and seven when Irene found out she was pregnant again. She was only thirty-six at the time, so she wasn't concerned about her risk for birth defects. That's why she expected her second sonogram to be fully routine.

But the doctor brusquely dropped a bombshell on her: "I saw many things on the sonogram that concern me. Your child has enlarged kidneys and long femurs, which could possibly be markers for Down syndrome or other problems with his chromosomes. If this child even lives through the pregnancy, I expect he would die in your arms shortly after birth. I recommend you see a genetic counselor and consider whether you should terminate this pregnancy."

Irene stared in shock, unprepared for both this detached delivery of news and its serious implications. Then she burst into tears, emitting a deep, guttural howl of grief. Her doctor was impassive, even impatient. He ushered her out of his office and quickly closed the door.

Blinded by tears, Irene barely drove home safely. She called her husband at the office and could only sob aloud into the phone. When Richard realized what she was trying to say, he rushed home to comfort her and to help her regain her composure before the kids got home from school.

In the ensuing weeks, Irene endured a number of tests. The results were always couched in terms of "a high percentage" or "quite likely" or "a strong possibility." But no one could give any guarantees that these tests were infallibly correct. Still, abortion was mentioned numerous times. "That's just not going to happen," Richard would say each time.

The day Irene went into labor, numerous prayer chains kicked into gear. On a warm spring day, she gave birth to Dean, a lively boy with bright blue eyes, blond hair, a mischievous sense of humor . . . and one slightly enlarged kidney. That's it, the sum total of his problems.

In fact, if anything, Dean is probably going to surpass his brother and sister, who are already enrolled in the gifted and talented program at their school. At three years old, his vocabulary routinely includes three-syllable words; he can spell his full name and count to ten; and he can climb up to the computer, click on the icon for the browser and then the icon for his on-line computer game, click to skip the ad, and play a game developed for children more than twice his age.

"Obviously, he is the delight of our family," Irene says. "He is very verbal and loves to tell us how much he loves each of us. We have very fond memories from last Christmas because of him. With each present he opened—no matter what it was—he'd announce the item and then add with a big squeal, 'It's just what I wanted!' And whenever I think of that, I think of those who assumed we would not want *him*. Those doctors were just so sure of their diagnoses that they would presume it was best to kill him. Sometimes I just want to take him to that first doctor's office and show that man how beautiful and healthy Dean is—and how very wrong he was in giving me such a horrific diagnosis."

Adopted, Not Aborted

*M*arty was married in her midthirties and didn't try to get pregnant right away. When she and her husband, Mike, decided it was time for children, they tried for six months. Since time was not on their side, they immediately started going to an infertility doctor. In fact, they went to several infertility specialists over three years. Finally, her doctor asked Marty, "Do you want to be pregnant or do you want to have a child?" And he pointed her toward adoption.

They tried one more time. "We were decided that if this didn't work, we were going to adopt," she said.

They were on their way to a beach vacation when the doctor called and said she wasn't pregnant. "I cried a lot on that vacation," she says. "I believed that God was able to make me pregnant—I read in the Bible that God would open the womb. So therefore I came to the conclusion that God had closed my womb because there were children that He wanted me to adopt."

Mike and Marty adopted their first boy, Lucas, from Romania; their daughter, Sandy, was a domestic adoption; Anton came three years later from Russia; and Saveta followed shortly, also from Russia. Some of their children came from difficult circumstances.

Mike and Marty had foster care of Sandy for three years before they could adopt her. Her mother was homeless and struggled with mental disabilities. She lived in Lafayette Park across from the White House before disappearing one year, never to resurface again.

Lucas's birth mother was in her fifth month of pregnancy, about to get an abortion. But one night, she had a dream in which she was told, "Don't abort the boy." She didn't know the sex of her child, but the dream sobered her enough that she immediately canceled the abortion and decided to give him up for adoption.

That was significant to Marty. "Ever since I was single, I would go to the annual March for Life in Washington, D.C. I was passionate about pro-life issues back then, but not as passionate as I was when I went through infertility."

Lucas was two years old in 1992 when Marty took him to his first March for Life. "As we walked, we encountered a whole section of pro-abortion feminists," Marty recalls. "They were angry and antagonistic about the rally. So I stepped up to them—holding Lucas—and said, 'I adopted him. Look at him! He could have been aborted.' I assumed they would be affected by this cute little boy, but it didn't affect them one bit. They shouted expletives in return. I was horrified by their reaction."

Lucas and his siblings have attended every March for Life since then, carrying signs saying, "I was adopted, not aborted." Often they are applauded. Sometimes they are jeered. In one recent march, his brother, Anton, was confronted by a group of self-proclaimed atheists who yelled at Marty for bringing her children, accusing her of forcing them to come and carry these signs. Anton immediately stepped up and corrected them, saying he wanted to come: "I believe in this. My life was spared! I definitely want to be here."

Then he witnessed to them, sharing the good news of Jesus' life, death, and resurrection.

"I think for my kids it's very meaningful to be in this march," Marty says. "They've seen the pictures of the babies who were aborted. They are very aware of how they were spared. Every one of my adopted kids could have been aborted. But their birth mothers all chose life and gave me the chance to adopt them. God has a purpose for them. I'm grateful. I always say to my kids, 'Your moms were poor and didn't have the money to take care of you. They could have aborted you, but they didn't. You can thank your birth moms that they went through labor and gave you birth.' God says we need to stand up for life. The Bible says we are to cry out for those who can't cry out for themselves—and that's what we're doing."

A Heart for Adoption

Roseanne grew up in a large Italian-American family, so when she and her sisters were children, they would often play at being mothers. Her younger sister would put a pillow under her shirt and pretend to be pregnant. Roseanne always pretended to adopt.

Roseanne met and married Anthony in her early twenties, and she quickly became a mother to four boys. From the beginning, they had planned to adopt. But after delivering her fourth child, Roseanne contracted a serious illness that put her on bed rest for a year. So all talk of adoption was put on hold.

When her youngest son was four, the family left New York and headed to a smaller town for Anthony's job. As she recovered, Roseanne continued to have a strong desire for adoption, but her husband wanted to wait until the boys were older and she had more strength. Roseanne was tempted to manipulate her husband, but God's grace helped her to be patient and trust Him. So she prayed . . . and waited.

Providentially, Anthony worked next door to an adoption agency. Two years after their move, he said it was time to start the paperwork.

"I was so excited. We both wanted to adopt a daughter—people have joked that we 'bought' a daughter—but adoption was on our hearts before we had any of our boys. And, in fact, they were all praying for a sister too," Roseanne recalls. "When we prayed, we always envisioned a mixed-race child, and that's what God provided."

Emilia joined their family two years after starting the adoption process. Her biological mother was white and her biological father was African-American; Emilia favored her mother, who had specifically requested Christian parents for her.

"We received Emilia when she was five weeks old, and it took about a year for the adoption to go through—but she was worth the wait," Roseanne says. "Emilia and I bonded immediately, a blessing I don't take lightly. She has always been my daughter, right from the start."

Her given name was Elizabeth, but that was also the name of Roseanne's grandmother, a woman who often expressed racial prejudices. Roseanne knew it would be better for everyone to rename her daughter.

"When my grandmother first heard about the adoption, she told me to go get a doll. She thought this would somehow appease this desire in me to have a daughter," Roseanne says, smiling. "My own parents tried to shield me from her deep prejudice—which, by the way, was prejudice against many other ethnic groups, not just African-American. My mother told me that this adoption was initially a struggle for my grandmother, but I never saw the struggle. In fact, one day my grandmother held Emilia, and I saw her kiss the baby on the forehead. I was stunned. My grandmother didn't even like to touch people of different races, but here she was kissing my little girl. God used my daughter to break my grandmother's ninety-year-old prejudice, and I believe she died a better person because of it."

As much as Anthony and Roseanne had prayed for and expected a mixed-race child, they still faced many unexpected learning curves.

"I can remember that with my other children, I bathed them daily and washed their hair. As an ignorant mother, I did the same thing with Emilia. One day a gracious African-American woman came over to me and asked me what I was doing to Emilia's hair. When I told her, she was horrified. She said, 'You can't wash African-American hair that often or it will become too dry and break off.' But I didn't know any better!" she says, chuckling at the memory.

Emilia is a young teenager now, but she still receives curious stares and awkward questions at times. "She wonders why she attracts this attention. When we go on vacation and go south, we've been pointed at and stared at in restaurants. Or when we go to the doctor, we'll get questions about how we're related. As she gets older, that bothers her more, which has led to good discussions. We've had to explain to Emilia that though we look a little different, we are the family that God has put together."

Roseanne also appreciates the candor of other adults, especially their African-American friends, who were initially concerned that the family would conform Emilia to white culture and wouldn't expose her to her black heritage. "I appreciated their honesty," Roseanne says. "We do want to make sure she has friends from many ethnicities, especially ones where she has the common bond of similar appearance. We want to expose her to many kinds of people."

Over the years, Roseanne has emphasized to her daughter that adoption is part of God's plan. "Through Jesus, we have been declared righteous in God's sight and are adopted into His family. It's an amazing privilege to be called a child of God! So we try to get Emilia to understand adoption is something very precious to God," she says. "Adoption is a part of the gospel message—and the gospel is the thing that unites all of us."

Grief and Grace

*T*alk about mixed messages. Elizabeth was five when her father moved out. Her parents were divorced shortly thereafter. She doesn't remember a lot about the divorce itself, but she does have clear memories of her divided childhood afterward.

"My mom had to work a lot after the divorce. We didn't have much fun around the house. I remember a lot of stress," Elizabeth says. "But my dad was the fun one, even though half the time he wouldn't show up as promised or pay the child support. My sister and I put up with the disappointment because we adored him. His actions didn't line up with his promises, but we just kept cutting him slack."

When Elizabeth and her younger sister did spend time with their father, they received a very strong message about what was important to him.

"My dad was with a different girlfriend every time we were with him, and they were obviously sleeping together," she recalls. "He was very big on being slim and looking good. It was about sex, basically, and how you looked. There was no moral influence on his end. From him, I learned that a woman needed to have a perfect body and be good in bed to keep a man. I don't think I thought much about homemaking or learning to cook as a way to please a man."

Elizabeth was twelve when her mother remarried. Her new stepfather was the exact opposite of her father. He was in the military and applied regimental discipline and order to their house. Her mother and stepfather were both committed Christians, but Elizabeth rebelled against them and their faith and became quite uncontrollable—even to the point of running away.

When she was a freshman in high school, she met Tony. He had dropped out of school and was working. They met through a mutual friend and Elizabeth was immediately dazzled. "He was the rebel guy, really rugged looking—just like my dad," she says, "but completely unreliable, given to lying. He cheated a lot on me and then would want to come back—and I would usually take him back. I thought I loved him. He would beg and cry, and I wanted to believe what he said was true."

She was sixteen when she became pregnant. She went to a Planned Parenthood clinic for the pregnancy test, and they immediately presented the option for an abortion. "When I left there, I was scared. I knew Tony would be upset that I was pregnant. I think we were on one of our 'outs' at the time, which is why I felt I had to handle this by myself."

The first person she told was her aunt, who encouraged her to tell her parents. Her dad immediately recommended an abortion. And so did Tony, when she finally told him. But her mother and stepfather helped Elizabeth to make the decision herself. Ultimately she decided against an abortion—much to her father's surprise and consternation. She decided to give the baby up for adoption to a Christian couple. "Even though I wasn't walking the Christian life, I wanted this child to have Christian parents," she says.

So Elizabeth's mother called an attorney she knew who handled private adoptions. While she was on hold, a woman named Lisa was talking to this attorney on the other line. He was delivering the bad news that the child Lisa wanted was going to another family—and that his pipeline for future adoptive children had dried up.

"This attorney had no other source. But Lisa replied, 'God is my source.' And of course, He was, for in the meantime, my mom was on hold on the other line to ask about adoption for my child. Lisa was totally right to trust God," she recalls.

"I was really young and scared, but I went ahead with the adoption. I knew that Tony would come in and out of my life, and I knew my son was going to experience the same thing with him that I had experienced with my dad. Of course, Tony was nowhere to be found until the end of my pregnancy. When I gave birth to Michael, he showed up drunk and didn't even stay or hold the baby. I was crushed, but I was so thankful to have my mom there. Immediately afterward, he made all kinds of threats about hiring an attorney, but just like I expected, it was just a bunch of noise."

Elizabeth had formed some attachment to the baby, so it was hard to give him up. Even though she knew it was the right thing to do, later on certain movies or events could trigger an unexpected flood of emotion. "But I will say that on the whole I had peace about it. It felt like the right thing to do. I always felt that he would be taken care of," she says.

Her attachment to Tony was even stronger, though, and eventually they got back together. The next few years were full of relational turbulence—they would date, break up, and reconcile all over again. The drama itself was addictive. Finally, they settled down. They had been together a solid year when they got engaged. Elizabeth was twenty-one, but she was in no hurry to marry. She wanted to wait five years, but Tony was pushing for marriage right away. That caused another rupture in their relationship, but Elizabeth was half-expecting it, anyway.

Not long afterward, a friend told her that Tony had gotten married. "I was shocked. I mean, we had been having a little trouble but we were *engaged*! The problem was, whenever we had problems, he would go back to his old girlfriend. And that's who he impulsively married behind my back."

And then there came the second positive pregnancy test.

"I just couldn't do it again," Elizabeth recounts with a heavy sigh. "Especially not with Tony now married to someone else."

Planned Parenthood was where she had the abortion. She was still in her first trimester. "It was awful. It hurt a lot and I was scared through the whole procedure. It was very different than the first time I was pregnant, when my mom was with me as I gave birth and was very supportive. The whole thing was so dirty and shameful."

Elizabeth was determined to break this cycle, so she moved across country away from Tony. After awhile, she moved in with her sister, who had gotten divorced from her husband. Both of them had been influenced by their mother's faith, but neither had professed any belief as young adults. So when her sister, Alesia, started going back to church, Elizabeth saw a profound change in her.

"It was a total turnaround in Alesia. I was fascinated. So I started going to church too. I had to see what was going on," she says. "One morning, I heard a sermon about God's purpose in salvation, and a switch just went off in my head. One moment I didn't believe, and the next moment—boom!—I did. I knew that all my sins, including the abortion, were covered by the blood of Christ the moment I repented and put my trust in Him. I felt so light and free, it was amazing!"

Elizabeth was twenty-eight at the time, eager to put her past behind her and live as a new creation in Christ. She was also a witness to the restoration of her sister's marriage—a milestone that Elizabeth treasured because she knew that God could really redeem sinful choices. At least other people's sinful choices—she harbored secret doubts that a godly man would want *her* because of her past.

Several years went by, but eventually a godly man did come along. They had been dating for about a year when Jack began to talk seriously about marriage. Elizabeth knew she needed to tell him about her past, but she wasn't sure how or when.

"I'd heard a message that those who have been forgiven much, love much. I felt so amazed at God's forgiveness for me, and I knew it would glorify God if I told Jack. The risk was that he might end our relationship. This was heavy on my heart at church one morning, and Jack could tell that I was affected. We were on our way to meet someone for lunch when he asked if I wanted to cancel. I burst into tears and he immediately pulled over. I didn't know how he would handle it, and I wasn't going to hold it against him if he couldn't," she says, crying at the memory.

"He was very kind, very gracious. He prayed for me, really ministering to me. I just wailed. It came from the depths of my soul. I was bawling but it didn't freak him out; he was kind and just so tender. He brought me back to the cross and the forgiveness I received there. He reminded me that this is where we all stand—equally sinful before a holy God."

Jack recalls that he felt something big was going to happen in that conversation, but he didn't know what it would be. However, he sensed an immediate resolve to support Elizabeth no matter what she said to him.

"Some things in life you get an opportunity to reverse, fix, or make right and some things you don't, but God's forgiveness is over it all," he says. "I remember us both grieving over her aborted child and rejoicing for the one who was still alive. It was a knock-the-wind-out-of-your-sails experience, definitely. There was grief, but there was also grace."

Less than six months later, Jack and Elizabeth were married. Being obedient to God, their honeymoon was the first time they were intimate with each other. The whole experience was beautifully redemptive for Elizabeth.

"It's amazing to be forgiven. I still marvel at God's kindness in all of it—including our marriage. I don't know if God will grant us children of our own, but maybe we will have a chance to adopt. I've been open to that for years. What a wonderful ending that would be to this testimony."

Seven

RAUNCH
Culture Rip-Off

*I*f you are under thirty, you may be experiencing the prover-
bial frog-in-a-pot-of-boiling-water scenario. What goes on
in our culture today may seem normal to you. It's not! Things have
changed so rapidly in just my lifetime that it's hard to comprehend.
My heart breaks for what some of you endure as a result of third-
wave feminism's impact on female sexuality. The current raunch culture is an utter rip-off for women. This chapter addresses the rise of
what is known as "porn-positive" or "sex-positive" feminism, and then
examines the celebration of real sex positivism as found in the Bible.
If you are sensitive to these matters, I've provided a summary at the
beginning of this chapter so you don't have to read further details,
even though I've labored to be as discreet as possible. And obviously
this is not a chapter suitable for young girls to read.

IT WAS THE LATEST POLITICAL scandal: a tough-on-crime
governor gets caught transporting a high-priced prostitute over state
lines. The media cranks up all the requisite snarky stories. The politi-
cian's wife is trotted out to glumly stand by her man as he admits to

what he was caught doing. After a few tense days, he resigns. As the porn industry makes the requisite million-dollar media appearance offers to the now-infamous call girl, the story seems about played out in the media cycle.

Fade to black; await the next scandal.

That is, until a staff member at one of those porn distributors realizes he could save his boss the money—for the producer of *Girls Gone Wild* already had sexual footage of this call girl when she was an eighteen-year-old on spring break in Florida. She loses her million-dollar offer; he likens the archival discovery to "finding a winning lottery ticket in the cushions of your couch."[1]

And millions of people who had never before seen nor heard of *Girls Gone Wild* are suddenly made aware of one of the prime showcases for the "female raunch culture" that arose in the third wave of feminism.

I had only heard of the show a few years earlier, when a critique titled *Female Chauvinist Pig: Women and Raunch Culture* by Ariel Levy was published in 2005. I was intrigued because I had not encountered anyone *within* the feminist movement standing up to say women were making horribly wrong choices in the name of sexual liberation. So I previewed the book on Amazon, where the featured chapter was about the author's experience with the *Girls Gone Wild* camera crew. Stunned by the description of the show, I shut down my browser. There was no way I could order the book. I was going to have to derive my understanding of Levy's thinking from magazine summaries and other secondhand sources.

This is also the challenge of this chapter. We live in a culture of hyperaggressive female sexuality, which is arguably the worst ever in recorded history. Those who promote this view often publish books and magazine articles with vulgar titles and references, stating that they are "reclaiming" these words for feminism. I find that I can't go to the original source for my research because I don't want to fill my mind or eyes with these descriptions and ideas, either. I exposed myself to it once before—as a college-age feminist—and I don't want to make that mistake again. Having been around the block a few times, so to speak, I used to think I couldn't be shocked.

I was wrong.

So I will try to be as discreet as possible in this chapter (challenging to do!), but if you just want to read the executive summary, here it is: God created sex. It is very good within His design. Outside of God's design, it inevitably causes problems. We are living in the fallout of that every day. Young women who are assaulted with "porn-positive" ideology of third-wave feminism are jaded, cynical, infected, and often deflated about these "freedoms." They are ripe to hear about God's plan for their sexuality. As Christians, we should not shrink from meeting them where they are and boldly demonstrating and proclaiming the gospel. We need to be able to discuss sexuality in candid but redemptive ways. We need to be clear that we are *not* antisex; rather, we are for the passion, trust, and enjoyment of marital sex as described in all its glowing celebration in Song of Solomon. The Judeo-Christian perspective celebrates female sexuality; therefore, we have all the more reason to pipe up when female sexuality is distorted and abused in our culture.

So if you are wondering why young girls wear "porn star" T-shirts, why the paparazzi offer twenty-four-hour coverage of the latest sex scandals of the "train-wreck" stars, why a local gym offers "strip aerobics," and why it's nearly impossible to find attractive yet modest clothing for yourself or your daughters—you are experiencing the effects, in large part, of third-wave feminism. "Sex-positive" or "porn-positive" theories are a large part of third-wave feminism. Third-wave feminists did an about-face, dismantling the opposition to pornography and sex work of the second wave by claiming participants in pornography and sex work can be "empowered." Third-wave feminists have also embraced a fluid concept of gender and rejected any universal definition of femininity.

Therefore, in this chapter, we will briefly track the rise of the raunch culture, the mixed messages of beauty and immodesty, and the extravagant grace that Jesus secured for our own sexual sins—and the sins of others against us.

Girls Gone Wild

Several years ago, writer Ariel Levy—who was born in 1974 in the midst of second-wave feminism and grew up on its logic—started to notice "something strange." Everywhere she went, it seemed pornography had gone mainstream, infecting mainstream TV, magazines, fashion, and entertainment. "Raunchy" had become synonymous with "liberated"—a trend that Levy found very confusing:

> Some odd things were happening in my social life, too. People I knew (female people) liked going to strip clubs (female strippers). It was sexy and fun, they explained; it was liberating and rebellious. My best friend from college, who used to go to Take Back the Night [feminist anti-sexual violence] marches on campus, had become captivated by porn stars. Only thirty years (roughly my lifetime) ago, our mothers were supposedly burning their bras and picketing *Playboy*, and suddenly we were getting implants and wearing the Bunny logo as symbols of our liberation. How had the culture shifted so drastically in such a short period of time?[2]

So Levy decided to research this trend, which included spending three days with the *Girls Gone Wild* video crew. In a nutshell, GGW cameras visited party spots like Mardi Gras or spring-break destinations, where they encouraged drunken young women to expose themselves or engage in sexual scenarios. The women who participated and the men who egged them on received either GGW T-shirts or trucker's caps. That's all they got—while GGW's founder, Joe Francis, earned millions from this footage. In one article, Levy quotes Mia Leist, GGW's twenty-five-year-old tour manager, saying, "people flash for the brand."[3]

Though heterosexual men are the obvious GGW audience, Levy says it no longer makes sense to just blame men. Women are not just in front of the cameras, they are also behind the scenes, making decisions, and making money:

> Playboy is a case in point. Playboy's image has everything to do with its pajama-clad, septuagenarian, babe-magnet founder, Hugh Hefner, and the surreal world of celebrities, multiple "girlfriends" and nonstop bikini parties he's set up around himself. But in actuality, Playboy is a company largely run by women. Hefner's daughter Christie is the chairman and CEO of Playboy Enterprises. The CFO is a middle-aged

mother named Linda Havard. The Playboy Foundation (which has supported the ERA and abortion rights among other progressive causes) is run by Cleo Wilson, an African-American former civil-rights activist. A woman named Marilyn Grabowski produces more than half the magazine's photo features. . . . That women are now doing this to ourselves isn't some kind of triumph, it's depressing.[4]

After spending three days with the GGW crew, Levy was more confounded than ever. "My argument is that women have forgotten that sexual power is only one, very limited, version of power and that this spring-break variety of thongs-and-implants exhibitionism is just one, very limited version of sexuality," she writes.

The marketing of this brand of female sexuality starts at a very young age. Wendy Shalit, author of *Girls Gone Mild: Young Women Reclaim Self-Respect and Find It's Not Bad to Be Good*, says that even six-year-old girls are affected by the intentional sexuality of Bratz dolls, "Hello Kitty" thong underwear, and suggestive clothing in the girls' department. As she writes, this kind of premature sexualization of girls is startling even to the pros:

> Across the political spectrum, many have expressed dismay that the legendary porn star Ron Jeremy was mobbed by families at Disneyland who wanted to have their picture taken with him, or that thirteen-year-old girls told the porn star Jenna Jameson at a book signing that they look up to her as an "icon." Reportedly, both Jeremy and Jameson were shocked to learn of their young fan base.
>
> But if we don't want this kind of thing to happen, then it seems that we need new role models. And we need them fast. For girls to have meaningful choices and genuine hope, the "wild girl" or "bad girl" cannot seem like the only empowered option.[5]

Unfortunately, many young women feel they have no other option in their relationships. Donna Freitas, a professor at Boston University and the author of *Sex and the Soul: Juggling Sexuality, Spirituality, Romance and Religion on America's College Campuses*, says that many of her students are unhappy with their own behavior when it comes to dating, romance, and sex. In her national college survey of more than twenty-five hundred students, Freitas discovered that 41 percent of those who reported "hooking up" (a range of sexually intimate activities unconnected to any committed relationship) were "profoundly upset about their behavior." The 22 percent of respondents who chose to describe a hookup experience (the question was optional) used words like "dirty," "used," "regretful," "empty," "miserable," "disgusted," "ashamed," "duped," and "abused" in their answers. An additional 23 percent expressed ambivalence about hooking up, and the remaining 36 percent were more or less "fine" with it, she reports.[6]

In her class, "Spirituality and Sexuality in American Youth Culture," Freitas assigned Wendy Shalit's book, *A Return to Modesty*, fully expecting her students to reject it. Instead, she reported that her students are "fascinated" by Shalit's description of modesty as a virtue, especially in the context of religious faith.

> The class was equally attracted to some evangelical dating manuals, like "I Kissed Dating Goodbye" by Joshua Harris and "Real Sex" by Lauren Winner, that I asked them to read. They seemed shocked that somewhere in America there are entire communities of people their age who really do "save themselves" until marriage, who engage in old-fashioned dating with flowers and dinner and maybe a kiss goodnight. They reacted as if these authors describe a wonderful fantasy land. "It would be easier just to have sex with someone than ask them out on a real date," one student said, half-seriously.[7]

This casual attitude toward sex comes with a high price. In March 2008, the Centers for Disease Control released a study that shocked many: An estimated one in four (26 percent) young women between the ages of fourteen and nineteen in the United States—or 3.2 million teenage girls—is infected with at least one of the most common sexually transmitted infections (human papillomavirus [HPV], chlamydia, herpes simplex virus, and trichomoniasis). The study also found that African-American teenage girls were most severely affected. Nearly half of the young African-American women (48 percent) were infected with a sexually transmitted infection, compared to 20 percent of young white women.[8]

The hookup generation not only has their sexual health and

future fertility at risk, they also are betting on a short-lived commodity: sexual attractiveness as defined by the porn industry. The leaders of third-wave feminism are now in their midthirties to early forties, and these younger women may soon appreciate the counsel of the generation ahead of them:

> At a spring 2008 conference at the University of Baltimore School of Law, academics, activists and students from around the country gathered to talk about feminism and societal change. There was some discussion of what distinguishes second- and third-wavers. When one young women's studies major asked what was wrong with drawing on her sexuality to gain power over men, one of her "elders" reminded her that such power was, at best, temporary, and that education and good employment might provide more lasting power.[9]

"Sex O'Clock in America"

Observing the social scene of young adults, a columnist for the *St. Louis Mirror* pronounced this era was "sex o'clock in America."

Reading that, would you assume the columnist was referring to today? The 1990s? The 1970s? How about the 1950s? Or the Jazz Age of the 1920s?

Would you believe 1914?[10]

Many of the same trends that characterized the closing years of the twentieth century were also present in its opening years. Marriage was on the decrease and divorce was on the increase. Between 1880 and 1913, the U.S. marriage rate hit its lowest point in the country's history to date. Divorce was also on the rise. In 1870, there were 1.5 divorces per one thousand marriages. By 1910, the divorce rate had risen to 5.5 divorces per one thousand marriages—the majority initiated by women.[11] And female sexuality was a hot topic in academia and the media.

By this period, the serious-minded "New Woman" of the suffragist period was being replaced by the forerunner of the Jazz Age's flapper. British sexologist Havelock Ellis had already published more than a dozen books on sexuality, including six volumes of *Studies on the Psychology of Sex*. Volume 3 addressed the sexual impulse in women, in which Ellis took the nineteenth century to task for assigning asexuality to women. "In ancient times men blamed women for concupiscence or praised them for chastity, but it seems to have been reserved for the nineteenth century to state that women are apt to be congenitally incapable of experiencing complete sexual satisfaction, and peculiarly liable to sexual anesthesia. This idea appears to have been almost unknown to the eighteenth century."[12]

Though no doubt we are glad to be rid of the nineteenth-century perspective on female sexuality, Ellis and his contemporaries set the stage for many of our current culture clashes.

In his candid autobiography, Ellis documented his own early impotence and open marriage with a feminist and lesbian, Edith Lees Ellis. His autobiography was one of more than two dozen books that he published on sexuality. He also supported the eugenics movement and served as the vice president for the Eugenics Education Society. His book on eugenics, *The Task of Social Hygiene*, promoted sex education in schools, saying that this reform—which he called sexual hygiene—"may well transform life and alter the course of civilization. It is not merely a reform in the class-room, it is a reform in the home, in the church, in the law courts, in the legislature."[13]

How right he was, unfortunately. In this book, he references Frau Maria Lischnewska, who promoted the idea that the school is not only the best way of introducing sexual hygiene, it is the only possible way, "since through this channel alone is it possible to employ an antidote to the evil influences of the home and the world."[14] Ellis predates the sex-education skirmishes of today by nearly a century.

It was during the years leading up to the Jazz Age that Ellis and another eugenics supporter, birth control advocate Margaret Sanger, had an affair. According to the Margaret Sanger Papers Project, "Sanger separated from her husband, William, in 1914, and in keeping with her private views on sexual liberation, she began a series of affairs with several men, including Havelock Ellis and H. G. Wells."[15]

The worldviews of Ellis and Sanger—and similar proponents—are part of the reason that today we have *Girls Gone Wild* and colleges offering "porn studies." According to author Nancy Pearcey, "the left-right split in American politics used to be over economic issues, such as the distribution of wealth. But today the split tends to be over issues of sex and reproduction: abortion rights, homosexual rights, no-fault divorce, the definition of the family, fetal experimentation, stem cell research, cloning, sex education, pornography."[16] Pearcey says that sexual liberation itself has become nothing less than a full-blown ideology:

> Sanger portrayed the drama of history as a struggle to free our bodies and minds from the constraints of morality—what she called the "cruel morality of self-denial and sin." She touted sexual liberation as "the only method" to find "inner peace and security and beauty." She even offered it as the way to overcome social ills. "Remove the constraints and prohibitions which now hinder the release of inner energies [her euphemism for sexual energies], [and] most of the larger evils of society will perish."
>
> Finally, Sanger offered this sweeping messianic promise: "Through sex, mankind will attain the great spiritual illumination which will transform the world, and light up the only path to an earthly paradise."[17]

Sanger lived to see the beginning of the "pornification" of America. She died in 1966, several years after *Playboy* began publication (in 1953) and Gloria Steinem wrote her famous exposé about being a Playboy Bunny (in 1963). This message to men was vastly different than what was distributed only a century earlier. As Glenna Matthews writes, "The point must be made that the contrast with the literature aimed at men in the [pre–Civil War] years could not have been greater. At that time, male readers had been cautioned that moral striving would be required before they could be worthy of the angels to whom they were wed. The tenor of advice to men after World War II was that they had a right to be self-centered and self-indulgent."[18] And *Playboy* was the most self-centered message of all.

Porn Goes Mainstream

Hugh Hefner launched *Playboy* from the kitchen of his Chicago apartment in 1953. He sold more than fifty-three thousand copies for fifty cents each—the beginning of a multimillion dollar enterprise. *Playboy* reached the height of its U.S. circulation in the early 1970s, shortly after it came under scrutiny by the Commission on Obscenity and Pornography, which was established by President Johnson in 1968. The commission published its report in 1970, stating that it found no evidence that pornography caused crime or delinquency among adults and youths. While it supported laws prohibiting sales of pornographic materials to children, it also recommended eliminating all legal restrictions on the use by consenting adults of sexually explicit books, magazines, pictures, and films.

At the same time, a serial killer named Ted Bundy began a horrifying murder spree across the country. From at least 1974 to 1978, he sexually assaulted and murdered dozens of young women in five states, dismembering and defiling their corpses in unmentionable ways. Some say he was responsible for more than one hundred such murders. He was sentenced to death in 1979 and spent ten years on death row before he was executed in 1989. He was one of the most notorious criminals in the twentieth century—as infamous for the extent and severity of his crimes as he was for his law-student smarts and boy-next-door good looks.

While Bundy was on death row, another national commission on pornography was formed in 1985 under President Reagan. Led by Attorney General Edwin Meese III, and informally known as the Meese Commission, this group included several prominent Christian leaders, including Focus on the Family's founder, James Dobson. In the sixteen years between these two commissions, society and technology had changed. The VCR had introduced porn films to private homes, but the Internet was not yet commonly available. Even so, there was a distinct difference in the way society viewed pornography from the 1970 commission to the Meese Commission:

> By this time, society had changed in several ways. Pornography had become even more available; a new generation of social science studies suggested a link between exposure to violent or degrading pornography and male aggression against women in laboratory settings; and new conservative and feminist movements were joining hands to attack pornography. In addition, the membership of the new commission was decidedly more conservative than that of the 1970 commission. Not surprisingly, the Attorney General's Commission on

Pornography, also known as the Meese Commission, reached strikingly different conclusions than did its predecessor. In its 1986 report, the commission concluded that violent pornography and degrading pornography (pornography showing the "degradation, domination, or humiliation" of women) cause violence and discrimination against women and an erosion of sexual morality.[19]

Here's the unusual twist: The language in this report of a "decidedly more conservative" commission bore a striking resemblance to many leading feminist statements of the time. What fascinates me personally is that I clearly remember this period myself. I had just graduated from college when the Meese Commission was formed. In my women's studies classes, I was taught the feminist position that pornography degrades women. I have forgotten many things about college, but the lecture about pornography is still clear in my mind because of the clarity of that argument.

The Porn Wars

Women Against Pornography coalesced in the late 1970s out of several feminist organizations, and it was loosely led by author Susan Brownmiller, who wrote *Against Our Will: Men, Women, and Rape*, and the militant activist Andrea Dworkin, among others.

Dworkin made headlines in 1980 for collaborating with feminist and legal scholar Catharine MacKinnon on behalf of Linda Lovelace, star of the X-rated movie *Deep Throat*, whose civil rights they were convinced had been violated. Dworkin campaigned frequently on the subject, helping to draft a law in 1983 that defined pornography as a civil rights violation against women. The law was later overturned by an appeals court as unconstitutional. Dworkin even testified before the Meese Commission and a subcommittee of the Senate Judiciary Committee, as reported in a 1979 *Time* magazine article:

> Perhaps the basic question is whether pornography really incites men to violence against women, or does the opposite—lets them sublimate their aggressive sexual fantasies in a relatively harmless way. The 1970 report of the President's Commission on Obscenity and Pornography

implied that it did indeed serve as a useful social outlet. But since then, at least one of the study's authors is having second thoughts. Says University of Pennsylvania Sociologist Marvin Wolfgang: "The weight of evidence [now] suggests that the portrayal of violence tends to encourage the use of physical aggression among people who are exposed to it." Backed by such support, Brownmiller and other feminists have every intention of stepping up their fight, hoping to recruit still more converts to their cause.[20]

Serial killer Ted Bundy could have been their poster child. In the final hours of his life before his execution in 1989 in Florida, Bundy gave a controversial video interview to Meese Commission member James Dobson. In it, he stressed over and over the influence of violent media and pornography on his thinking, and on the thinking and impulses of the other men in prison with him. "I've lived in prison for a long time now and I've met a lot of men who were motivated to commit violence, just like me. And without exception, every one of them was *deeply* involved in pornography—without question, without exception. Deeply influenced and consumed by an addiction to pornography. There's no question about it. The FBI's own study on serial homicide shows that the most common interest among serial killers is pornography."[21] Bundy claimed he wanted to make this warning about pornography his final message because he had seen the mainstreaming of porn and he was concerned for future generations.

Opposition to pornography was the link between two groups that typically had little else in common: the Christian Right and feminist activists. For a brief period in 1980s, they found themselves on the same page. It wasn't a comfortable alliance for feminists. It began when Dworkin and MacKinnon wrote a civil rights ordinance introduced in Minneapolis in 1983 that allowed any woman to bring a civil suit against the makers and distributors of pornography. It was passed by the Minneapolis city council but was vetoed by the mayor.

The next year, this ordinance was introduced to the Indianapolis city council by a conservative Republican who had hired MacKinnon as a consultant. During the Indianapolis hearings, the antiporn feminists were supported by the conservative Christian groups, the Moral Majority, and Eagle Forum. As one historian noted, "The anti-pornography movement was now aligned, although not happily or for the same reasons with the conservative pro-family forces that had been active in anti-feminist causes since the mid-1970s."[22] Nor did all self-identified feminists support the antiporn activism.

> The movement quickly ran into trouble. In 1983, the members of WAP pushed forward a ban on pornography in Minneapolis, which they hoped would serve as a national model. Suddenly, their support dropped through the floor. To many, the campaigners began to look like puritans who were taking things too far, and free-speech activists rose up with a shout. Finally, a few young women emerged with shocking news: They liked pornography.[23]

The "porn wars" were the last gasp of second-wave feminism. As the sexual liberation message collided with the victimhood message, the resulting contradiction led to serious infighting. As Ariel Levy explains, the antiporn faction of feminist leaders "felt they were liberating women from degrading sexual stereotypes and a culture of male domination and—consequently—making room for greater female sexual pleasure. [Their] opponents thought they were fighting a new brand of in-house repression. . . . Everyone was fighting for freedom, but when it came to sex, freedom meant different things to different people."[24]

Concurrently, porn was becoming more mainstream—first through the VCR and then through the Internet. Just as the Jazz Age daughters of New Woman suffragists rebelled against the relentless seriousness of their mothers and their causes, so did the daughters of "patriarchy is the problem" second-wavers. The result was the "sex-positive" or "porn-positive" feminism that arose in the third wave of the early 1990s. It hinges on the idea that sexual freedom is essential to women's freedom, and it opposes all legal or social efforts to control or limit sexual activities. According to one definition, sex-positive feminists reject the vilification of male sexuality that they attribute to many radical feminists of the second wave, and instead "embrace the entire range of human sexuality," including gay, lesbian, bisexual, and transgendered sexuality.

"Real Women Are Bad Porn"

Some argue that today's raunch culture is a reaction to the omnipresence of pornography. In order to get and keep a man's attention, women feel that they have to act and look just like porn stars. According to a *New York* magazine article, one Manhattan-based sex therapist says that she's seen many young men coming in to chat about Internet porn-related issues. "It's so accessible, and now, with things like streaming video and Webcams, guys are getting sucked into a compulsive behavior," she says. "What's most regrettable is that it can really affect relationships with women. I've seen some young men lately who can't get aroused with women but have no problem interacting with the Internet. I think a big danger is that young men who are constantly exposed to these fake, always-willing women start to have unreal expectations from real women, which makes them phobic about relationships."[25]

Feminist writer Naomi Wolf agrees. "The ubiquity of sexual images does not free *eros* but dilutes it," Wolf writes. "Today, real naked women are just bad porn."[26]

Twenty years down the line from the "porn wars" of second-wave feminism, Wolf notes that part of what was forecasted then has come true now—and part was wrong. In an article titled "The Porn Myth," Wolf writes of running into antiporn feminist Dworkin at a benefit, which caused her to reflect on what Dworkin had once prognosticated.

> If we did not limit pornography, she argued—before Internet technology made that prospect a technical impossibility—most men would come to objectify women as they objectified porn stars, and treat them accordingly. In a kind of domino theory, she predicted, rape and other kinds of sexual mayhem would surely follow. . . .
>
> She was right about the warning, wrong about the outcome. As she foretold, pornography did breach the dike that separated a marginal, adult, private pursuit from the mainstream public arena. The whole world, post-Internet, did become pornographized. Young men and women are indeed being taught what sex is, how it looks, what its etiquette and expectations are, by pornographic training—and this is

having a huge effect on how they interact.

But the effect is not making men into raving beasts. On the contrary: The onslaught of porn is responsible for deadening male libido in relation to real women, and leading men to see fewer and fewer women as "porn-worthy." Far from having to fend off porn-crazed young men, young women are worrying that as mere flesh and blood, they can scarcely get, let alone hold, their attention.[27]

Peanut Butter and Jelly

As I was writing this chapter, I met a fifteen-year-old girl who had not been exposed to Christian thinking about sexuality. Her sexual experiences to date in her young life are jaw-dropping—and my concept of saving sex until after marriage is equally as foreign to her. She was initially attracted to the idea of men treating women with respect and honor, but when she found out part of that was due to the delayed gratification of sexual activity, she couldn't fathom it. She thought for sure something was wrong with men who could exercise that kind of self-control. And since marriage has not been a future expectation, either, she has had no particular reason to decline the most base offers for group sex and other hookup sexual activity.

I've been thinking a lot about her as I've worked on this material. Her notion of sexuality and relationships breaks my heart. Her acceptance of how she's been treated by men—who, I might add, have committed a crime because she is a minor—breaks my heart, as well. Though she is an extreme example, she is not uncommon. To her and her friends, sex is a transaction that you negotiate and then discard. I don't know if I will have any opportunities to talk with her again in the future, but I pray I do. There are many things I want to talk to her about, including the Christian perspective on sex.

As I mentioned earlier in the book, I didn't become a Christian until I was thirty. I lived a liberated lifestyle, you might say, until that time. My understanding of the Christian perspective of sex was "just say no." So I was pleasantly surprised as a new believer to hear pastors and women's ministry speakers teach openly about God's good gift of sex. They weren't inappropriate, but it was refreshing to hear an unblushing celebration of marital sex being presented to the church. As

C. J. Mahaney writes in his book to Christian husbands:

> It is regrettable that when it comes to sex, secular culture sees Christianity as concerned primarily with prohibitions. Obviously, sin regularly corrupts God's good gift of sex by divorcing it from the covenant of marriage and trying to create a counterfeit experience. All misuse of sexuality is condemned in Scripture. The Bible's warnings against immorality and the power of lust must never be denied or ignored; so it's right that we keep them clearly in mind. Even in Solomon's Song we find repeated admonitions against premature sexual activity (2:7; 3:5; 8:4).
>
> But once joined in marriage, things change, guys! In the beginning, God looked upon the erotic union of husband and wife and saw that it was good. His opinion has not changed in the slightest. . . . Sex was created for marriage, and marriage was created in part for the enjoyment of sex.[28]

This is a message that needs to cut through our porn-saturated media. The timeless solution is the one-on-one mentoring model. The Bible instructs older women to teach younger women how to love their husbands, be self-controlled, and pure (Titus 2:4–5). Purity is not only for the time before marriage but also the time afterward: "Marriage should be honored by all, and the marriage bed kept pure, for God will judge the adulterer and all the sexually immoral" (Hebrews 13:4 NIV). I believe pastors should be teaching the church on Sundays what the Scriptures say about sex, but the one-on-one settings make room for the candor, questions, and confessions that elude the larger crowds.

We need to combat any false notions of sexuality and piety by presenting a clear and unblushing portrayal of marital intimacy. A generation that is well acquainted with the physical variations of sex needs to hear about the powerful security, attraction, and emotional freedom that attend monogamous marital fidelity. Young women who are constantly disrespected by men need to hear how marriage is built upon mutual respect and honor—and how that should make a wife feel cherished and prized. They also need to know that God is not ashamed of what He created. "Even though it's intensely physical, it is not the least bit unspiritual," Mahaney writes. "When a married couple is in the midst of enjoying sexual relations, they may not be experiencing holiness in the same way they experience it when praying or worshiping God, but make no mistake—that is a very holy moment. It is God's desire that every Christian couple . . . regularly enjoy the best, most intimate, most satisfying sexual relations of which humans are capable."[29]

In the popular media, married sex gets no applause. If it is referenced at all, it is the stuff of dull jokes. This is why personal mentoring is important. Older women who have successfully weathered the various seasons of marriage need to give practical sexual counsel . . . such as making peanut butter sandwiches for dinner—a timeless tip from C. J. Mahaney's wife, Carolyn:

> Recently I had a conversation with a young first-time mother. "Before our baby was born," she explained, "I had plenty of time to romance my husband, clean my home, and cook delicious meals. But now there are days I'm still in my bathrobe at three o'clock in the afternoon, because I've spent all morning caring for our newborn! So how do I keep my husband a priority when my child requires so much time and attention?" she asked.
>
> "Honey," I replied, "fix your husband a peanut butter and jelly sandwich for dinner and give him great sex after dinner, and he will feel prized by you!"[30]

As older women mentor younger women in God's design for sexuality, it also presents an opportunity to circle back to basic issues like modesty in clothing and emotional expression.

"His Banner Over Me Is Love"

A girl putting on an immodest outfit will think she just looks good—because that's what fashion dictates. Her outfit may not be the true reflection of her values, but it's what she can buy. So she continues to add to the daily accumulation of the raunch culture's visual impact. In the same way, I think many young women imitate porn stars (on a variety of levels—from dress to personal grooming to relationships) because it's what they believe is attractive to men. If it's "hot," it must be good. In the absence of other teaching, there is a certain perverse logic to this.

That's why we must proclaim without apology the beauty of modesty and restraint. As one of my married male friends tried to explain to my sexually active fifteen-year-old acquaintance: "The price of a candy bar is one dollar because that's all that it costs to get it. You don't pay two dollars because you don't have to; one dollar is sufficient. Well, the price of my wife was everything I had and then some. She was not going to part with the treasures of her sexuality, her affections, her romance, and her support apart from my pledging my life and love to her until death do us part. She was priceless, in some ways. And I knew that going in—she demanded my respect and honor. And it's been completely worth it."

Author Wendy Shalit says that modesty today is always taken to be shame, although they are two distinct words and two different concepts. "The prevailing view is that if you think sexuality should be private or special," she writes, "then you must be ashamed of it. You're a prude. Conversely, if you are 'comfortable with your sexuality,' then you should be 'cool' with lifting your shirt for strangers or cheering on your man as he enjoys a lap dance with another woman. If you're like me, you may wonder how this harem mentality is liberating for women."[31]

The Bible's erotic love poem, the Song of Solomon, repudiates the idea that modesty and a lack of sexual passion are interconnected. Instead, the husband in this poem is clearly smitten by his wife's sexual appeal: "You have stolen my heart, my sister, my bride; you have stolen my heart with one glance of your eyes, with one jewel of your necklace. How delightful is your love, my sister, my bride! How much more pleasing is your love than wine, and the fragrance of your perfume than any spice!" (Song of Songs 4:9–10 NIV). Yet he also speaks of her sexual purity and modesty prior to marriage: "You are a garden locked up, my sister, my bride; you are a spring enclosed, a sealed fountain" (v. 12). As Daniel Akin writes in *God on Sex*, this sexual restraint was what made their marital lovemaking so passionate:

> To other men she was locked up, enclosed, and sealed. For her husband she is wide open, accessible, and available. Indeed, her love is

overflowing and streaming for him. What she once held back from others she now gives to her husband with unreserved passion and abandonment. And why? Because she had saved herself for this day and this man. She was no casualty of sexual promiscuity. She did not have the wounds of a young twenty-one year old who said with pain and sadness in her voice, "I have had seventeen partners—too many, I think." Purity and pleasure go hand in hand when it comes to sex. Be specific in your availability. It is worth the wait.[32]

I long for young women to understand this principle. It is natural for us to want to captivate a man's attention. But a *Girls Gone Wild* T-shirt is no symbol of love. It's simply a badge of a tawdry performance. It conveys no lasting security or honor or even attraction.

The bride in the Song of Solomon speaks of something far more precious: "He has taken me to the banquet hall, and his banner over me is love" (Song of Songs 2:4 NIV). This bride has received public affirmation and acclaim, and she wears her husband's love like a banner. Instead of insecurity or disappointment, this woman revels in her status: "Strengthen me with raisins, refresh me with apples, for I am faint with love" (v. 5). She is no hookup casualty or discarded sexual partner. She is celebrated and prized—and intoxicated with her husband's sexual attention.

This is the message that young women today need to hear. God's original design for sex is still the best.

THE SAVIOR OF SUNSET BOULEVARD

THERE ARE MANY MORE issues to explore than there is space in this book. "Sex work" is one of them. Even before the "porn wars" divided feminism, there was a contingent trying to decriminalize prostitution to improve conditions for sex workers. While some sex workers in developed nations may choose to enter this profession, many thousands more around the world are victims of human trafficking for sex tourism.

Here is a testimony of a woman who was a prostitute during the time some second-wave feminists began to campaign for decriminalized sex work. She did engage in prostitution of her own free will, but she did not remain in prostitution of her own free will. That's an important difference—and one I suspect is true of many more women like her. The first time I heard her testimony, I was shocked. Never in a million years would I have thought this quiet, gentle woman who loved country crafts and worship music would have once walked the streets of Hollywood. But that's the amazing transforming work of God's grace. He does indeed make us new creatures in Christ.

Jen was around five when her parents divorced. She was the youngest of five children, with two older sisters and two older brothers. The divorce split up the family; from that point on, she never lived again with all of her siblings.

It wasn't long before her mother remarried. Jen's stepdad was a lot like her biological dad: both were alcoholics. Though the family was fairly dysfunctional, as she recalls it now, Jen is grateful that no one ever abused her, physically or sexually.

She grew up in Little Rock, Arkansas, rotating through living arrangements with her mom, her dad, and her older sister. No one in the family had a lot of money, but they always had time to party. Watching the lifestyle of the adults around her, Jen decided that she would be different.

"I was one of those kids who used to say I would never smoke, drink, or cuss," she recalls. "Of course, those were the three things I ended up doing. I started getting high around age twelve or thirteen. So in some sense, my parents did try to steer me in the right direction, but if they weren't going in the right way themselves, what could they do?"

When she was very young, the family periodically visited a Pentecostal church in a little Arkansas town. Then when she was twelve or so, Jen visited a Baptist church with her mom and stepdad. "I remember at different times throughout my life thinking, *Is God real? Is there a heaven or hell?*"

During her junior year of high school, Jen was living with an older sister and working part-time. She didn't like school and her grades had declined. "There was no real authority figure in my life," she says. "So I just quit school and started working full-time as a waitress."

That was where she met Kevin, a well-known pimp. "There were pimps and prostitutes who came into this restaurant all the time," Jen recalls. "I was looking at it from the outside and seeing the 'glitter' in it—the nice clothes, the nice cars, the easy money. I was somewhat fearful about it all, but it still drew me. I was also a little bit familiar with the lifestyle because my sister had been a prostitute for a while, though not when I was living with her. So in the end, the appeal outweighed the fear."

At the time Jen began dating Kevin, he already had one prostitute working for him. Kevin's father was a pimp, too, though his mother was not a prostitute and remained married to him. None of these facts deterred Jen. "I liked him from afar before we got involved," she says. "Kevin had charm. He was nice. He dressed well. He was attractive."

Dating him led to the expectation of working for him. Jen was attracted to Kevin and believed she loved him, so she agreed. "The first time was in Texas. There was this certain area where the girls would work. You would wave or say, 'You want a date?' I was fearful. When I was with these men, I would steel myself against it because I didn't like it. I didn't like them touching me. I wanted it over as quick as possible. In Texas, I would have to get in the car with a man and drive somewhere. So I'd have to ride with them and hope they wouldn't do anything weird."

Jen was only with Kevin for less than a year, but she was arrested and jailed a number of times for prostitution in Arkansas, Texas, and California. "The vice squad would come along and put fear in the prostitutes. I remember the police in Texas seemed to really care, trying to talk us into leaving that life."

Two months into their relationship, Kevin began to physically abuse Jen. She would leave him, but then she would always come back for reasons that are unclear to her even today.

"I think the thing that drove me the most was fear of Kevin. If I didn't make enough, he would be upset. Crazy things could set him off," she says. "The last time he physically abused me, we were in California together. He took an iron and hit me on the side of my head, and I had to get stitches in my ear and I had two black eyes. I didn't work for about a week. The day I went back, I wasn't doing well. I didn't make much money that day. There was no trust left. I really thought he would kill me."

Jen never kept any of the money she made—it all went to Kevin, despite all the risks she took. One time when she was out on the street, she was raped. Another time, a guy pulled a gun on her. A third man actually came looking for her with a gun. "All this happened in less than a year on the street. My sister was in it for many years—what must she have gone through?" Jen asks sadly.

One night Jen was working on Sunset Boulevard, near Hollywood. She had heard about Centrum, a homeless mission for prostitutes, runaways, and other women on the streets. She wanted to go there to escape Kevin, but she was immobilized by the fear of his retribution. In desperation, she prayed a quick prayer, "God, send someone to help me."

That very night, someone from Centrum came by, handing out tracts for the mission. Jen couldn't believe it. So she asked to be taken in. At twenty-two, she was ready to leave the streets.

The next night at Centrum was a testimony and worship night. During that meeting, Jen couldn't stop crying. The house mom, a woman in her sixties, noticed her reaction and called Jen into her office to share the gospel. They ended up praying together for Jen to repent of her sins and receive the Lord.

Centrum was affiliated with Youth With a Mission (YWAM), which enabled Jen to leave California after two months and transfer to a YWAM center in Colorado. She really wanted to get away from everything that reminded her of Kevin and her former life. She can't imagine any other reason than God's protection that kept Kevin away from her.

Eventually, Jen moved to another YWAM center in the East and was there for several years, working in various YWAM training centers. She eventually left YWAM for full-time employment. At the same time, she had joined a new church and developed a new circle of friends. Her quiet demeanor and YWAM credentials led many to assume she had grown up in a Christian family, going to church every week and leading a relatively sheltered life. Jen discreetly held her tongue about her background.

One year, she was invited by a family in the church to spend Christmas with them. They had also invited another single adult, a man named Matt. Jen had noticed Matt when she first came to the church, thinking that he had gentle eyes. But she didn't expect him to notice her. Matt was the good boy—the one who became a Christian in high school through a Young Life outreach and never smoked, drank, or used drugs. He was also a virgin, waiting for marriage to experience sex with his wife. Jen couldn't imagine that he'd still be interested in her if he knew the truth about her.

Amazingly, they clicked. Over the next several weeks, they had various reasons to get together—a singles hike, a movie night. On an unusually warm February day, Matt took her on a picnic to a city park that was known for its romantic settings. Jen held her breath as he began to talk to her about his feelings—she couldn't believe he wanted to pursue a relationship with her.

The next steps would require great wisdom. When should Matt know about her past? And how much should he know? Jen paid a visit to her assistant pastor and his wife to get their counsel. Her pastor said that Matt should know before engagement, but it was still too early in their relationship for him to be in her confidence. He would stay in touch with Matt and let her know when the time might be right.

One day, Matt got the call. "I remember my pastor calling me and saying, 'Jen has some stuff she needs to tell you. You need to get together,'" he recalls. "So I called Jen and she said, 'I don't know if you are going to want to continue on after hearing this.' And so obviously I wasn't going to sleep after hearing her say *that,* so I went over that same night."

Jen was calm, but she could hardly bear to look Matt in the eyes. When she was finished, she looked up at him and said, "I would understand if you broke up with me. I want you to know that. You don't have to stay with me if you don't have faith for it."

Matt was initially shocked, but it only took a moment for him to look at her with compassion. "I would never have guessed any of this," he said. "God has changed you so much, Jen. Your past is not who you are today. Therefore, if God has forgiven you and accepted you, who am I to think any differently? It would be my honor to represent Christ to you and to love you and serve you like Christ does."

They were married six months later.

Fifteen years later, Matt and Jen are now the parents of three children. A dozen red roses sit on the coffee table in honor of their anniversary. Jen sits close to Matt, smiling up at him as he speaks of their courtship and engagement.

"Matt is never reluctant about me talking about my past," Jen says. "He is not ashamed of me. He wants God to get the glory."

Matt nods as she says this. "God had prepared my heart—He had given me a sense that she was someone God had accepted and I had no right not to do so. Sometime during our courtship, I had an impression that God was speaking to me. Essentially it was, 'Jen is My daughter and if you wrong her, you will have to deal with Me.' And that's something that still applies today. I have a responsibility before God to treat His daughter well."

Turning to look at his wife, he adds with a laugh: "So I'm surprised He hasn't come down already!"

In her story, Jen mentioned being physically abused. I think it is important to point out that this is a sin in God's eyes, and the church needs to respond biblically and thoroughly to this issue. While physical and sexual abuse historically has been a concern within feminist circles (and with good reason!), it is not an exclusively feminist topic, so I did not address it as such in this book. However, I do want to point you to the appendix, where there are two brief articles that clearly state a gospel-centered, Bible-based perspective about abuse.

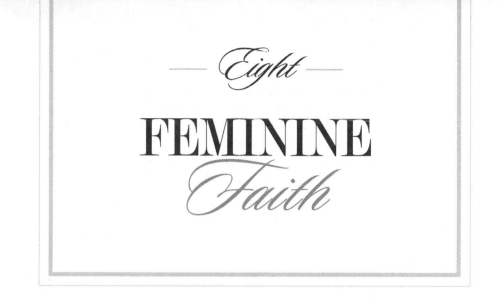

Eight

FEMININE
Faith

This is truly an overview chapter. There is so much more information about the impact of feminism on the church than I could ever include here. In fact, entire tomes have been written about this topic. I recommend that you check out the endnotes if you want a list of resources for further reading. In this chapter, I merely want to introduce you to some of the issues and to urge you to become women who are immensely fruitful for God's glory! As we'll see, only "one thing" is truly needed in the eyes of Jesus, and the woman who chooses it will not see it taken away from her.

AT A RECENT CONFERENCE for pastors, theologian and fellow pastor John Piper received a spontaneous and heartfelt round of applause when he began to fervently preach about the worth of strong women: "I love strong women! I think they are magnificent testimonies to Christ. Because if they are complementarian—which I hope they are at our church —then they are combining things the world can't explain. They are combining a sweet, tender, kind, loving, submissive, feminine beauty with this *massive* steel in their backs and theology in their brains!" he said. "I grope for ways to celebrate and articulate such *magnificence* in women."

Of the 5,300 people assembled, the vast majority were men. Yet few things at the conference roused such a thunderous response than this assessment of strong women. When he said it, Piper tempered his comments with a facetious remark that people often misunderstand this perspective, "because John Piper hates women, don't you know that?"[1]

Why did he say this? Because of the term he used, "complementarian," which refers to men and women occupying complementary roles while being equal in value. Piper—like the rest of the pastors assembled at this conference—believes that the Bible is to be read plainly and taken seriously when it says that men are to lead the church (and lead their families). Due to his teaching on this topic, Piper has been a lightning rod for criticism and misunderstanding.

In the twenty-first century, few things are more controversial than the Bible's plain teaching on sexuality and gender roles.

There are, in my opinion, at least three reasons for this controversy. One is that within the church, we have forgotten that the role of leaders is "to equip the saints for the work of ministry, for building up the body of Christ" (Ephesians 4:12). We have become consumers within the church, requiring professional service of pastors to serve *us*—rather than becoming a mobilized body of servants to care for each other and those outside of the church. When the church is operating biblically, everyone is needed for the purpose of ministry— not just the "professional class." Another reason is our celebrity culture: whoever is in the position of speaking publicly is deemed to have more worth than the one who is serving quietly behind the scenes—the opposite of what Jesus taught (Matthew 20:25–27). So if there is any restriction in the public role, it is seen as inherently wrong because everyone should be able to have a shot at it, even if the Bible makes it clear that only a few are gifted and qualified to lead the church (1 Timothy 3). The third reason is the influence of feminism on church life and theology, which is the focus of this chapter.

As we've seen throughout this book, feminist ideology arose from partially accurate observations but offered faulty interpretations and flawed solutions. Unfortunately, in evaluating and debating these interpretations and solutions, those who hold to the complementarian position have not always responded to the valid observations feminists have made. As theologian Steven Tracy noted, these concerns should have stimulated immediate action:

> If feminists have identified legitimate concerns, they must be fiercely addressed. Sadly, while biblical complementarians oppose the abuse of male leadership, they have been extremely slow to address specific issues of male abuse in a detailed fashion. . . . We should consider it utterly unbiblical for men to dishonor women, as we consider it utterly unbiblical to deny worship to Christ. Just as we would be offended at and oppose the teaching of anyone who would deny that the Father raised Christ from the dead and will eschatologically vindicate him, so we should be deeply offended that anyone would fail to honor and protect women.[2]

So while we look at the history of feminism's influence on the church itself, I want to acknowledge once again that wherever human beings exist, there will be sin and imperfection. The big picture is not how well human beings have performed but what God says about Himself, His church, and His design for His creatures. I would be unwise to point to the track record of those who espouse complementarian roles as the standard of behavior and approach. In humility, we must admit that there's been failure on both sides—but that will never negate God's Word.

Therefore, we need to clearly and unapologetically embrace the Bible's teaching on manhood and womanhood. "The church should lead the way in equipping God's people to think biblically about all of life, including a biblical perspective of gender roles and relationships," write Ligon Duncan and Susan Hunt in their book on women's ministry. "Scores of evangelical women are functional feminists, because the world's paradigm for womanhood is the only one they have ever heard."[3]

Fumbling the Gospel

It may be surprising to look back from our postmodern, religiously pluralistic culture and note that the issue of church leadership was one of the major factors for the rise of feminism. But as we saw in chapter 2, the earliest feminists listed grievances against the church in the same document as grievances against mainstream institutions.

As a movement, feminism has its roots in the post-Enlightenment period that challenged traditional institutions, customs, and morals. The authority of the (male) clergy was one of those challenged institutions. In addition, the Second Great Awakening also influenced the rise of feminism. This nineteenth-century revival movement emphasized personal spiritual experience and personal conversion, but one of its key leaders also rejected many core Christian doctrines. Revivalist Charles Finney denied that the righteousness of Christ is the sole ground of our justification and that Christ's death on the cross was atonement for our sins.[4] Finney was known for leading emotional, lengthy crusades that thousands attended. (You may recall from chapter 2 that early feminist Elizabeth Cady Stanton attended a number of his revival meetings and then rejected orthodox Christianity.)

These revival meetings attracted more female than male converts and adherents. One reason may have been that Finney allowed women to pray aloud in mixed settings, an unusual practice at that time. While there is nothing in Scripture that prohibits women from praying aloud in church, unfortunately that soon led to an unbiblical acceptance of ordaining women. Because women historically had been largely excluded from participating in church life, when the door opened to proclaim the gospel and share in the spiritual harvest, it's understandable that they would associate that kind of ministry with the pastorate. However, based on the New Testament pattern where *all* members are called to various forms of ministry, this kind of spiritual fruitfulness is not limited to leaders. Nevertheless, spiritual fruitfulness eventually became one of the reasons given for allowing women to preach to mixed audiences or to become ordained pastors.

To justify their ideas, first-wave feminists used two primary methods of interpreting Scripture. First, early feminist writers countered the argument of those who limited the leadership role of women by citing passages that spoke of the equality of men and women in Christ. (But as we've noted before, equality and role are not equivalent concepts.) Second, they celebrated women in Scripture who could serve as role models for female leadership, such as Deborah,

Ruth, or Esther. By the end of the nineteenth century, feminists began to label certain biblical texts as demeaning to women and challenged their authenticity. We saw this in chapter 2 with Elizabeth Cady Stanton and *The Woman's Bible*, which was really more of a commentary on selected passages regarded as significant for women.[5]

The problem is that when you begin to selectively believe and apply only certain Scriptures—or disbelieve or ignore them as irrelevant—it's very easy to continue doing so with other passages until you have gutted Christian doctrine. The first woman ordained in a mainstream denomination—Antoinette Brown Blackwell—is a good example. She was ordained by a Wesleyan Methodist leader in 1853 and ended her career as pastor of a Unitarian church. Her father had been converted under Finney's teaching, but Blackwell did not believe what Finney said about hell. "I was greatly impressed by his graphic doctrine of eternal punishment," she wrote. "I seemed to believe it but even at that day had no real faith in it."[6] Theological confusion created even more theological confusion.

Mary Kassian, the author of *The Feminist Mistake*, says that when feminism developed and the inequities in women's participation were highlighted, the church lost an opportunity to rightly restructure church patterns. Instead of seeking to recapture New Testament patterns and dissolve the artificial distinction between clergy and laity, she says the church chose to retain its current structure and open up the avenues of ordained ministry to women as well as men:

> Unfortunately, Christian feminists began to pursue the inclusion of
> women in leadership hierarchies without a clear analysis of whether or
> not the hierarchies themselves were structured and functioning according
> to a biblical pattern. They merely judged the church to be sexist
> and implemented a course of action in response. Christian feminists,
> alongside their secular counterparts, began to demand "equal rights."
> They decided to seek androgyny in the church by pursuing women's
> ordination and the obliteration of structured roles in marriage.[7]

The nineteenth century witnessed an enormous number of challenges to historic Christian theology. It is beyond the scope of this book to untangle and describe them here. But in general, as liberalism began to take over segments of the church, feminism had an open door. Liberal theology, according to one author, is "the idea of a Christian perspective based on reason and experience, not external authority, that reconceptualizes the meaning of Christianity in the light of modern knowledge and ethical values."[8] Or, more simply put, liberal theology denies the authority of the Bible, the atoning work of Jesus Christ, and many other core doctrines of Christianity even as it embraces the popular philosophies of its time. The rise of liberalism eventually led to the twentieth-century division of American Christianity into liberal mainline churches and conservative evangelical and fundamentalist churches.

Woman-Centered Spirituality

With liberalism having created a form of Christianity without many of its central doctrines, the door was wide-open for alternative spirituality to emerge, which discarded any pretense of Christianity. By the middle of the twentieth century, when second-wave feminism began, leading feminists began to deny any belief in Christianity, monotheism, or traditional religion. By the 1970s, it was common for secular feminists to embrace alternate spirituality, such as Wicca (witchcraft). As Mary Kassian writes, "The so-called 'male-defined male' God of the Judeo-Christian religion was unacceptable to a woman-centered analysis of reality and to the female quest for spirituality. Therefore, feminist women decided to discard Him."[9] In God's place, many feminists adopted a homegrown blend of goddess worship and witchcraft designed to promote spiritual energy for the movement. "Feminism had always been, in essence, a religious movement, and now it was openly recognized as such," Kassian notes.[10]

It wasn't long before this same pagan worldview infiltrated Christian circles too. I clearly remember the "Re-imagining God" conference that took place in Minneapolis in 1993. I was a brand-new Christian then and read the press coverage with interest. More than two thousand national leaders from twenty-seven nations and fifteen mainline denominations attended, including ordained leaders, to "listen to the god within," worship the goddess Sophia in a milk-and-honey communion, and discuss the idea that Jesus' atonement was "the ultimate in child abuse." Their argument was that the death of Jesus Christ is not a work of salvation but that it encourages social violence and particularly violence against females.

Eventually, evangelicals started down the same path. Wayne Grudem argues that evangelical feminists are now making some of the same arguments that liberal, mainline feminists once made. "In a surprising number of evangelical feminist writings, the authors have published statements that either deny the complete truthfulness of Scripture or else deny the full authority of Scripture as the Word of God for us today," Grudem writes.[11]

These are not linear trends I've just outlined but more an interconnected web that has at its root an altered gospel. As soon as one aspect of the Bible is doctored, then it's not long before key doctrines crumble and the gospel is fumbled. Today, many church leaders feel the pressure to conform to current cultural trends by not upholding male leadership in the church. I pray the witness of history will encourage both these pastors and their members to reconsider this slippery slope of Bible tampering.

Only One Thing Is Needed

Jesus said that only one thing is needed.

I believe that when we forget His words, we easily lose our bearings about gender roles. We either swing from unbiblically limiting women to certain spheres or we swing to the other side of saying there is no distinction between men and women. Without the "one thing," we make too much of ourselves, shoving and pushing for fleeting earthly status and recognition.

What I'm referring to is the biblical account when Jesus and His disciples come for rest and refreshment in the home of two apparently single sisters, living with their brother. One sister, Martha, takes seriously her responsibility to provide hospitality to this important group of visitors. But she grows irritated that her sister, Mary, is sitting with the men at the feet of Jesus to hear Him teach. So she begins to grumble about her sister—finally blurting out sinful judgment against both Mary and Jesus: "Lord, don't you care that my sister has left me to do the work by myself? Tell her to help me!" (Luke 10:40 NIV).

Without demeaning her hospitality or the importance of domesticity, Jesus gently rebukes Martha. He says, "Martha, Martha . . . you are worried and upset about many things, but only one thing is needed. Mary has chosen what is better, and it will not be taken away from her" (vv. 41–42). In other words, worshiping the Lord and listening to Him speak always trumps our other roles and efforts. It is good to offer hospitality, but it is *far better* to do so with a heart of worship than a heart of worry. When we compare and contrast our service and our roles among each other, we take our eyes off of Jesus and start judging Him ("don't you care?") rather than worshiping Him.

In allowing a woman to sit at His feet to hear Him teach, Jesus was breaking some of the norms and practices of Jewish culture. But those were man-made laws that relegated women to certain sections of the temple or kept them from active ministry. Jesus did not keep these unbiblical prohibitions, but He did keep the clear teaching of Scripture about roles in marriage and spiritual leadership. He taught women, He received physical sustenance and financial support from women (see Joanna, for example), and He addressed women who were shunned by others or would be ignored by Jewish men (see the Samaritan woman at the well). As theologian John MacArthur says, this was in stark contrast to other men of Jesus' day:

> In the midst of the Greek, Roman and Jewish cultures, which viewed women almost on the level with possessions, Jesus showed love and respect for women.
>
> Though Jewish rabbis did not teach women, Jesus not only included women in His audiences but used illustrations and images in His teaching [that] would be familiar to them (Matt. 13:33, 22:1–2, 24:41; Lk. 15:8–10). He also specifically applied His teachings to women (Matt. 10:34f).
>
> While the Jewish Talmud said it was better to burn the Torah than teach it to a woman, Jesus taught women freely. To the Samaritan woman at the well (Jn. 4), He revealed that He was the Messiah. With her He also discussed such important topics as eternal life and the nature of true worship. Jesus never took the position that women, by their very nature, could not understand spiritual or theological truth.

He also taught Mary and, when admonished by Martha, pointed out the priority of learning spiritual truth even over "womanly" responsibilities like serving guests in one's own home (Lk. 10:38–42).

Though men in Jesus' day normally would not allow women to count change into their hands for fear of physical contact, Jesus touched women to heal them and allowed women to touch Him (Lk. 13:10f; Mk. 5:25f). Jesus even allowed a small group of women to travel with Him and His disciples (Lk. 8:1–3)—"an unprecedented happening in the history of that time," said one commentator.

After His resurrection, Jesus appeared first to Mary Magdalene and sent her to announce His resurrection to the disciples (Jn. 20:1–18). Jesus did this despite the fact that women were not allowed to be witnesses in Jewish courts because they were all believed to be liars.[12]

Jesus corrected these false standards of behavior among the religious of His day and then pointed us to the one thing that is really needed for men and women—to worship Him. When we lose sight of that, even the good things we do to serve Him become temptations for sinful comparisons and self-righteous anger—just as it did for Martha. This is especially true as we consider roles within the church. Even though Jesus did much to correct the status of women in His day, *the one thing He did not do was select a woman for a position of leadership.* Jesus affirmed the equality of men and women while also supporting the biblical design of complementary roles.

The apostle Paul followed his Lord's example by colaboring with women in many aspects of proclaiming the gospel—from evangelizing Lydia in Philippi (Acts 16:14–15) and founding the first European church in her home to entrusting Phoebe with delivering his letter to the Romans (Romans 16:1). But he did not appoint women to the roles of pastors or elders, writing under the inspiration of the Holy Spirit that a woman must not teach or have authority over a man (1 Timothy 2:11–12).

If this stirs up resentment in our hearts, I believe that's because we've lost sight of the gospel. We deserve punishment for our sins (a very unpopular thought in our postmodern culture), but if we worship Jesus, it is because we have received forgiveness and mercy instead— *and this for all of eternity!* Does it really matter how our Lord asks us to serve Him for just a few short years on this earth when we will equally delight in Him for time without end?! Even those men who are called to be pastors will only serve in that position for a portion of their lives. All the good things we can do here on earth are trumped by the one thing that is truly good—to worship Jesus now and for all of eternity! We have received far better than we deserved, thanks to the mercy of the cross. Let us not quibble about the small part we play in advancing Christ's kingdom and the good news of salvation.

Faith in Action

In conclusion, I would like to take you back to those heady moments in the nineteenth century when women were being included in church life and social reform was a pressing matter. As the first wave of feminism was gaining momentum, there were small bands of Christians who looked at injustice, inequity, and poverty and decided to meet these problems head, on *with the gospel.* They were Christians who went out as part of the first wave of American missionaries to other nations—sent by the fledgling organization, the American Board of Commissioners for Foreign Missions (ABCFM).

My ancestors were among them. At age twenty-two, Amos Abbott and Anstice Wilson were married in Wilton, New Hampshire. He was a graduate of Andover Theological Seminary with an assignment to teach at a mission school in Amednugger, India. Eleven days after their wedding, they sailed for India. Their journey from Boston to Bombay in 1834 required about four months of ocean travel through rough waters. A civil war was in progress when the Abbotts reached India, but they persevered.

For the next twenty years, the Abbotts ministered in India and raised seven children. Anstice Abbott started a school for her children and the children of other missionaries too. Eventually the family returned to America in order to provide their children with a good education and allow Amos to get a medical degree. While they were back home in the United States, one of their daughters, Augusta, met one of the students her father was tutoring in the Marathi Indian dialect— Samuel Dean. After a brief courtship, Samuel asked Augusta to join him in India to continue the family's work. Just like her mother,

Augusta was married, and the couple put out to sea in a matter of days. In those days, families said a final good-bye to each other, not knowing when or if they would see each other again. So her parents told Augusta good-bye and sent their daughter back to India.

Samuel proved to be an effective preacher and church planter. In addition to conducting regular preaching services and organizing new churches near his own home, Samuel often journeyed into the remote sections of India where people had never heard the name of Christ—and Augusta often went with him. Sometimes they camped for days, with snakes and bubonic plague an ever-present danger. Eventually this hard work wore down Samuel, and the family returned to America in 1867 so Samuel could recover his health. He went on to be a church planter in Nebraska for the next dozen or so years before he died.

In 1889, Augusta found herself a widow in a changing world. Many controversies were shaking the nation and the church, but Augusta decided to go back to India. She wanted to work with her sister, Annie, who ran a home for young Hindu widows. Because the girls would marry very young in India, many of the widows were practically children. Since the widows were considered disgraceful in Indian culture, these young women were shunned by society and their own families. The home that Annie ran protected these widows, gave them a basic education, and schooled them in a marketable craft. The older widows who attained sufficient proficiency in reading were known as the "Bible Women"—a point of controversy in the Hindu culture.

The Dean and Abbott influence was felt in this section of India. When Augusta returned a second time to India, she was greeted shortly thereafter by an Indian man who had searched for her, hearing that the widow of the great preacher Samuel Dean was nearby. He was waiting to tell her how fruitful Samuel's preaching had been, for now there were several churches in the region that sprung from his preaching. And he wanted to pay his respects to the widow of the great Samuel Dean.

Augusta spent nearly five years working with the "Bible Women" there before she returned home. In an age when transoceanic travel was hard work, she made the trip to India twice to face down Hindu intimidation and teach important life skills to abandoned widows.

Augusta was a very spiritually fruitful woman. All of her children became Christians, and she left a rich spiritual heritage to them. She was a fearless helpmate to her husband, working with him to found churches in two nations. She ran her own home, educated many children (including her own), and still served women from another culture who were wrongfully discarded within their own society. Augusta's letters indicate a bright, headstrong, and outspoken woman. She could have pushed for many things for herself, but she deferred to her husband's gifting and helped him be as successful as possible.

I often wonder about her, my grandmother's grandmother and sister in the Lord. She could have been influenced by first-wave feminism, but she chose another path. She saw inequity and injustice in India, and chose to meet that need through the gospel. She could have enjoyed her retirement in relative ease in the United States, but she chose to give away her life to those who desperately needed help. And when she returned to India, she received the good news of the fruit of her colabors with her husband. Together, they accomplished much—and by all accounts, together they stayed true to the glorious gospel.

A Call to Radical Womanhood

Augusta lived more than one hundred years ago, but she was an example of the strong women that John Piper celebrates, women who "combine sweet, tender, kind, loving, submissive, feminine beauty with this *massive* steel in their backs and theology in their brains." It takes a formidable woman to travel twice under difficult circumstances to a nation hostile to her spiritual message. It takes a strong woman to selflessly nurture four children into adulthood. It takes a spiritually mature woman to follow her husband in his calling and support him in his gifting, traveling to the other side of the world to help him carry out his plans. It takes a bold woman to live counter to her culture, choosing the glory of Christ above any personal honor.

It's my joy to honor Augusta's memory. She was truly a radical woman, a woman whose feminine expression of faith stood the test of time in a feminist world. She honored the institution of marriage, she delighted in bearing and rearing the next generation for Christ, she was faithful to her marriage vows, and she sat at the feet of Jesus in order to receive from Him what she needed to give to countless others who had never before heard His name.

May God grant each of us the grace to do the same—and may this be our spiritual legacy for the women who follow in our footsteps!

APPENDIX:
Resources on Abuse

he issue of abuse—be it physical, verbal, or sexual—is worthy of a separate book itself. I do not feel qualified to address this topic in depth, but I do want to point you to two important resources that have been reprinted with permission. The first is a statement on abuse from the Council on Biblical Manhood and Womanhood (CBMW). This statement dispels any notion that those who hold to the complementarian perspective of male and female roles would in any way condone abuse. The second resource is a brief article from Ken Sande, the president of Peacemaker Ministries. This ministry provides outstanding counseling and conflict resolution resources for both the individual and the local church. In this article, Sande addresses a painful reality in some churches and offers a biblical response.

Council on Biblical Manhood and Womanhood's Statement on Abuse

When CBMW was founded in 198, its leaders wrote in the Danvers Statement that "we have been moved in our purpose by the following contemporary developments [that] we observe with deep concern." Among the items listed was "the upsurge of physical and emotional abuse in the family." At that time, CBMW leaders also committed themselves to work as a council:

- to bring healing to persons and relationships injured by an inadequate grasp of God's will concerning manhood and womanhood,
- to help both men and women realize their full ministry potential through a true understanding and practice of their God-given roles,
- and to promote the spread of the gospel among all peoples by fostering a biblical wholeness in relationships that will attract a fractured world.

In addition, the Danvers Statement affirmed that:

- In the family, husbands should forsake harsh or selfish leadership and grow in love and care for their wives.

CBMW continues to grieve over the alarming rise in abuse in its many forms, and recognizes a need for a fuller, stronger declaration of our conviction that the Bible speaks clearly and forthrightly against abuse and that it speaks with equal clarity on the differing responsibilities of men and women in marriage.

Therefore, the Council has issued an expanded statement on abuse as part of a continuing effort to demonstrate that the biblical teachings on male headship in marriage do not authorize a man's domination or abuse of his wife.

We hope this statement will encourage Christians to oppose abuse wherever it appears.

Adopted by the Council on Biblical Manhood and Womanhood at its meeting in Lisle, Illinois, in November 1994.

Statement on Abuse

- We understand abuse to mean the cruel use of power or authority to harm another person emotionally, physically, or sexually.

- We are against all forms of physical, sexual, and/or verbal abuse.

- We believe that the biblical teaching on relationships between men and women does not support, but condemns abuse (Prov. 12:18; Eph. 5:25–29; Col. 3:18; 1 Tim. 3:3; Titus 1:7–8; 1 Pet. 3:7; 5:3).

- We believe that abuse is sin. It is destructive and evil. Abuse is the hallmark of the Devil and is in direct opposition to the purpose of God. Abuse ought not to be tolerated in the Christian community.

- We believe that the Christian community is responsible for the well-being of its members. It has a responsibility to lovingly confront abusers and to protect the abused.

- We believe that both abusers and the abused are in need of emotional and spiritual healing.

- We believe that God extends healing to those who earnestly seek Him.

- We are confident of the power of God's healing love to restore relationships fractured by abuse, but we realize that repentance, forgiveness, wholeness, and reconciliation is a process. Both abusers and abused are in need of ongoing counseling, support, and accountability.

- In instances where abusers are unrepentant and/or unwilling to make significant steps toward change, we believe that the Christian community must respond with firm discipline of the abuser and advocacy, support, and protection of the abused.

- We believe that by the power of God's Spirit, the Christian community can be an instrument of God's love and healing for those involved in abusive relationships and an example of wholeness in a fractured, broken world.

A BETTER WAY TO HANDLE ABUSE

by Ken Sande, president of Peacemaker Ministries

SEXUAL ABUSE IN THE CHURCH DOES not have to end in broken lives, ago-nizing lawsuits, and divided congregations. When people follow God's ways and words, these terrible incidents can result in healing, justice, and health-ier churches.

When victims of abuse first come forward, I have found that most of them are seeking four reasonable responses. First, they are looking for un-derstanding, compassion, and emotional support. Second, they want the church to admit that the abuse occurred and to acknowledge that it was wrong. Third, they want people to take steps to protect others from simi-lar harm. And fourth, they expect compensation for the expense of needed counseling.

As national headlines reveal, many churches have unwisely ignored these legitimate needs. Instead, like many other institutions, they have blindly fol-lowed their lawyers' and insurance adjusters' textbook strategy to avoid legal liability. They try to cover up the offense and deny responsibility. All too often they distance themselves from the victims and their families, leav-ing them feeling betrayed and abandoned.

Many frustrated victims eventually talk to a lawyer who tells them they could win a million-dollar damages award. Soon everyone is locked in an adversarial process that reopens wounds and generates even more pain and anger. Whatever the verdict, both sides lose, since money alone can never heal the wounds of abuse.

There is a better way.

God is a redeemer and a problem-solver. He has designed a powerful peacemaking strategy for dealing with offenses between people, including sexual abuse. When churches follow it, as I will show later, the cycle of abuse is broken and restoration can begin.

COMPASSION—If there is one place that victims of abuse should find understanding, compassion, and support, it is among people whom God commands to respond to suffering with tenderness and selfless love: "Be kind and compassionate to one another. . . . Do nothing out of selfish ambition or vain conceit. . . . Each of you should look not only to your own interests, but also to the interests of others" (Eph. 4:32; Phil. 2:3–4). Instead of pulling away from victims, churches should draw closer to them, listening to their stories, mourning with and praying for them, and bearing their burdens. Responding with love and compassion is one of the best ways to show that the church abhors abuse and is committed to serving those who are suffering.

CONFESSION—Attorneys instinctively instruct their clients to "make no admissions." Hundreds of churches have followed this shortsighted counsel in recent years, prolonging the agony of abuse victims, infuriating juries, and triggering multimillion-dollar punitive damages awards. In contrast, everyone benefits when people trust God's promise that "he who conceals his sins does not prosper, but whoever confesses and renounces them finds mercy" (Prov. 28:13). When abuse has occurred, a church should express sorrow and acknowledge its contribution to the situation. It should also counsel the abuser to confess his sin, take responsibility for his actions, and seek needed counseling. These steps can prevent a court battle and speed healing for victim and offender alike. (Since an impulsive admission could allow an insurer to cancel coverage, church leaders should consult with their insurer, lawyer, and a Christian conciliator to plan their words carefully.)

COMPENSATION FOR COUNSELING—The Bible places a strong emphasis on requiring a wrongdoer to repair any damage he has caused to another person. "Pay the injured man for the loss of his time and see that he is completely healed" (Ex. 21:19). Therefore, churches should be earnest to do whatever they can to bring wholeness to victims of abuse. As soon as abuse is revealed, the church should immediately come to the aid of the victim and his family, holding forth the redeeming power of Jesus and offering to provide or pay for needed counseling.

CHANGE—When abuse takes place, statements of regret are not enough. Genuine repentance is demonstrated by making changes to protect others from similar harm. "Produce fruit in keeping with repentance. . . .

Rescue the weak and needy; deliver them from the hand of the wicked" (Luke 3:8; Ps. 82:4). This requires immediately removing the abuser from his position, involving legal authorities as needed or required by law, and implementing screening and supervision procedures to prevent other abusive people from being in counseling or child-care positions. Such actions not only protect others from harm but also relieve abuse victims, who are deeply concerned that others not be treated as they were.

CONCILIATION—It may be difficult for a church to implement these steps if a victim's family is already threatening legal action or an insurer refuses to support personal contacts. These situations can still be resolved without a legal battle, however, by submitting the matter to biblical mediation or arbitration. "If you have disputes about such matters, appoint as judges even men of little account in the church!" (1 Cor. 6:4). Christian conciliation by outside neutrals can provide a constructive forum to deal with both the spiritual and legal issues related to abuse. This legally enforceable process provides appropriate confidentiality and promotes confession and restitution, which help to bring about justice and reconciliation.

These five steps are not theoretical. I have seen many churches follow this process, usually with great success. In one case, a pastor discovered that a man had abused several children in the church, including the pastor's daughter. In the midst of his own personal anguish, the pastor prayed to respond to the situation in a way that would reflect the love of Jesus. After consulting with a Christian conciliator and the church's insurer, the pastor and his elders set out to minister to everyone who had been hurt by this dreadful sin.

They persuaded the abuser to confess his sin to the families of the children and to turn himself in to the police. He willingly accepted his prison sentence, and was even grateful that his destructive behavior had finally been stopped.

The leaders spent many hours with the families themselves, grieving and praying with them, and making sure they received needed support and counseling. In addition, the leaders improved their screening and supervision policies to guard against similar incidents in the future.

They also reached out to the abuser's wife and children, who were so ashamed that they planned to leave the church. But the leaders understood what being a shepherd is all about. They ministered to this broken family, reassured them of God's love, and kept them in the fold.

Instead of being dragged through an excruciating lawsuit, the victims and their families, the abuser and his family, and the entire congregation experienced the redeeming power of God. This remarkable process culminated months later during a Christmas Eve service. As the church prepared to sing "Silent Night," two young girls came forward to light the candles. One of them had been abused. The other was the daughter of the abuser. As they finished their task and smiled at each other, the congregation saw tangible evidence of God's love and grace.

Abuse in the church does not have to end with catastrophe. When a church follows its Lord, even this great tragedy can result in healing and restoration.

© Peacemaker Ministries. Reprinted with permission. (For more information about biblical peacemaking, visit www.peacemaker.net.)

ACKNOWLEDGMENTS
and Thanks

To Lesley Mullery and Nicole Whitacre at Sovereign Grace Church of Fairfax, who first asked me to develop a message on feminism and biblical womanhood—and kindly hung in there during the review process.

To the First Draft Team—friends and family members who faithfully read my initial drafts and gave me feedback—Mickey and Jane Connolly, Saralyn Temple, Ashleigh Slater, Diane Martinelli, Heidi Michaelian, Jan Lynn, Isaac Hydoski, Erin Sutherland, Katherine Reynolds, Ben Wright, Sarah Lewis, Joanna Breault, Alice Barber, Ken Barbic, and Kim Wagner. Special honor goes to my parents, James and Rosalind McCulley, who were always the fastest members of the review team and the most encouraging.

To Megan Mattingly and Bethany Gill for their research assistance.

To my bosses at Sovereign Grace Ministries, Pat Ennis and Bo Lotinsky, who graciously accommodated my shifting work schedule to complete this project.

To C. J. and Carolyn Mahaney, who faithfully prompted me for more than a year to develop this book and make it a priority.

To Nancy Leigh DeMoss, who interviewed me about this topic for her radio show and then gave me a deadline of her own conference in order to get it completed. Thank you for the introduction to Moody!

To Jennifer Lyell at Moody Publishers, the most simpatico editor a girl could ever want. May you get the Jimmy Choos of your dreams! Thanks for your endless support and enthusiasm for this book.

Finally, to all those who allowed me to use their stories in this book—your God-glorifying lives literally speak volumes. For the sake of those who will read this book and benefit from your example, thank you for your humility.

NOTES

Chapter 1: Dented Feminity

1. Roger Woolger and Jennifer Barker Woolger, *The Goddess Within: A Guide to the Eternal Myths That Shape Women's Lives* (Ballantine, 1989), 44, 47.
2. Richard L. Ganz, *20 Controversies That Almost Killed a Church* (Phillipsburg, NJ: P & R Publishing, 2003), 155.

Chapter 2: Men Aren't the Problem

1. Charles Francis Adams, *Familiar Letters of John Adams and His Wife Abigail Adams, During the Revolution* (New York: Hurd & Houghton, 1875), 149–50.
2. Lynne Withey, *Dearest Friend: A Life of Abigail Adams* (New York: Touchstone Books, 1981), 82.
3. "The Declaration of Sentiments," as archived on the National Park Service's historical archive, http://www.nps.gov/wori/historyculture/declaration-of-sentiments.htm.
4. From the supporting materials on the PBS website for Ken Burns's documentary about Elizabeth Cady Stanton and Susan B. Anthony, *Not for Ourselves Alone*, http://www.pbs.org/stantonanthony/resources/index.html?body=dec_sentiments.html.
5. The Smithsonian Institution's National Portrait Gallery, online education materials at http://www.npg.si.edu/col/seneca/senfalls1.htm.
6. Marilyn Yalom, *A History of the Wife* (New York: Perennial Publishing, 2002), 190.

7. Glenna Matthews, *"Just a Housewife": The Rise and Fall of Domesticity in America* (New York: Oxford Univ., 1987), 138.

8. Elizabeth Cady Stanton, *Eighty Years and More* (Humanity Books, 2002), 43.

9. Ibid., 44.

10. Elizabeth Cady Stanton, *The Woman's Bible*, 1898, as posted on the Sacred Texts website at http://www.sacred-texts.com/wmn/wb/wb02.htm.

11. Yalom, *History of the Wife*, 121–22.

12. Ibid., 145.

13. Hazel Rowley, *Tete-a-Tete: Jean-Paul Sartres and Simone de Beauvoir* (New York: HarperCollins, 2005), 28.

14. Louis Menand, "Stand by Your Man: The Strange Liaison of Sartre and Beauvoir," *New Yorker*, September 26, 2005,http://www.newyorker.com/archive/2005/09/26/050926crbo_books.

15. Simone de Beauvoir, *The Second Sex* (New York: Vintage Books, 1989), xix.

16. Mary Kassian, *The Feminist Mistake* (Wheaton: Crossway Books, 2005), 22.

17. Gemma O'Doherty, "Simone de Beauvoir was the mother of feminism . . . and on her centenary, all they write about is her scandalous love life," *Irish Independent*, January 12, 2008, archived on http://www.independent.ie/.

18. Diane Johnson, "The Life She Chose," *New York Times*, April 15, 1990, http://www.nytimes.com/books/98/12/06/specials/bair-simone.html.

19. Ibid.

20. O'Doherty, "Simone de Beauvoir".

21. Søren Kierkegaard, quoted in "Existentialism," article in Microsoft Encarta Online Encyclopedia 2008, http://encarta.msn.com.

22. Betty Friedan, *The Feminine Mystique* (New York: W. W. Norton, 2001), 18.

23. Ibid., 32.

24. F. Carolyn Graglia, *Domestic Tranquility* (Dallas: Spence Publishing, 1998), 13.

25. Patricia Sullivan, "Voice of Feminism's 'Second Wave,'" *Washington Post*, February 5, 2006, http://www.washingtonpost.com/wp-dyn/content/article/2006/02/04/AR2006020401385.html.

26. Kate O'Beirne, *Women Who Make the World Worse* (New York: Sentinel, 2006), 20.

27. Ibid., 21.

28. Marilyn Gardner, "Betty Friedan: A Dynamo for Women's Rights," *Christian Science Monitor*, February 7, 2006.

29. Margalit Fox, "Betty Friedan, Who Ignited Cause in 'Feminine Mystique,' Dies at 85," *Washington Post*, February 5, 2006.

Chapter 3: "Did God Really Say . . . ?"

1. Gloria Steinem quotes, collected on the Women's History page of About.com, http://womenshistory.about.com/cs/quotes/a/qu_g_steinem.htm.
2. Associated Press wire story, "Feminist Icon Gloria Steinem First-Time Bride at 66," September 5, 2000, http://archives.cnn.com/2000/US/09/05/steinem. marriage.ap/index.html.
3. Gloria Steinem quotes, collected on Thinkexist.com, http://thinkexist.com /quotes/gloria_steinem.
4. Gary Martin, "The Phrase Finder", http://www.phrases.org.uk/meanings/414150. html.
5. Gloria Steinem, "Women's Choice", *Washington Post*, January 18, 2002, http:// discuss.washingtonpost.com/wp-srv/zforum/02/nation_steinem011801.htm.
6. As written in the "Ask Amy" column on Feminist.com, May 2003, http://www. feminist.com/askamy/feminism/503_fem8.html.
7. Jennifer Baumgardner and Amy Richards, *Manifesta: Young Women, Feminism, and the Future* (New York: Farrar, Straus & Giroux), 2000, 61.
8. Melissa Denes, "Feminism? It's Hardly Begun," *The Guardian* (UK), January 17, 2005, http://www.guardian.co.uk/g2/story/0,3604,1391841,00.html.
9. Sam Roberts, "51% of Women Are Now Living without Spouse," *New York Times*, January 16, 2007; http://www.nytimes.com/2007/01/16/us/16census.html.
10. Andreas J. Köstenberger with David W. Jones, *God, Marriage, and Family* (Wheaton: Crossway, 2004), 25–26.
11. Ibid., 165.
12. Ibid., 170.
13. Wayne Grudem, *Evangelical Feminism and Biblical Truth* (Sisters, OR: Multnomah Publishers, 2004), 46–47.
14. Ibid., 25–26.
15. "The Wedding Song," by Noel Paul Stookey, 1971.

Chapter 4: Role Call

1. Robert Lee Hotz, "Deep, Dark Secrets of His and Her Brains," *Los Angeles Times*, June 16, 2005, http://www.latimes.com/news/science/la-sci-brainsex16jun16,0, 5806592,full.story?coll=la-home-headlines.
2. Kassian, *Feminist Mistake*, 58.
3. Greg Behrendt and Liz Tuccillo, *He's Just Not That into You* (New York: Simon Spotlight Entertainment, 2004), 16–17.
4. Ibid., 79.

5. Pew Research Center Social and Demographic Trends, "As Marriage and Parenthood Drift Apart, Public Is Concerned about Social Impact," July 1, 2007, http://pewsocialtrends.org/pubs/526/marriage-parenthood.
6. Jennifer Roback Morse, "Why Not Take Her for a Test Drive?" published on Boundless.org, http://www.boundless.org/2001/departments/beyond_buddies/a0000498.html
7. Judy Syfers, "Why I Want a Wife," *Ms.*, spring 1971, http://www.feministezine.com/feminist/modern/Why-I-Want-A-Wife.html.
8. Grudem, *Evangelical Feminism and Biblical Truth*, 119.
9. Jennifer Roback Morse, "Husband's Day," *National Review Online*, June 16, 2006, as archived on http://nationalreview.com.
10. John Ensor, *Doing Things Right in Matters of the Heart* (Wheaton: Crossway Books, 2007), 97–98.
11. Gary Thomas, *Sacred Influence* (Grand Rapids: Zondervan, 2006), 79.
12. John Piper and Wayne Grudem, *Recovering Biblical Manhood and Womanhood* (Wheaton: Crossway Books, 1991), 61.
13. John Piper, "Marriage: Pursuing Conformity to Christ in the Covenant" sermon, delivered to Bethlehem Baptist Church, February 25, 2007, http://www.desiringgod.org/ResourceLibrary/Sermons/ByDate/2007/2006_Marriage_Pursuing_Conformity_to_Christ_in_the_Covenant/.
14. Carolyn Mahaney, "Watch Your Man" message, Sovereign Grace Ministries Leadership Conference 2005, as archived on www.sovereigngraceministries.org.
15. C. J. Mahaney, recorded remarks to the Sovereign Grace Ministries Pastors College, March 2008, as presented on the Sovereign Grace Ministries blog, http://www.sovereigngraceministries.org/Blog/post/How-to-Help-Your-Husband-When-Hes-Criticized.aspx.
16. Phyllis Schlafly, *Feminist Fantasies* (Dallas: Spence Publishing, 2003), 234–35.
17. Carrie L. Lukas, *The Politically Incorrect Guide to Women, Sex, and Feminism* (Washington, D.C.: Regnery Publishing, 2006), 97.
18. Köstenberger, *God, Marriage and Family*, 234–35.
19. Thomas, *Sacred Influence*, 60–61.

Chapter 5: There's No Place Like Home
1. Linda Hirshman, "Homeward Bound," *American Prospect*, November 21, 2005, http://www.prospect.org/cs/articles?articleId=10659.
2. Ibid.
3. Ibid.

4. Linda Hirshman, *Get to Work: A Manifesto for Women of the World* (New York: Viking, 2006), 2.

5. Linda Hirshman, "Unleashing the Wrath of Stay-at-Home Moms," *Washington Post*, June 18, 2006, http://www.washingtonpost.com/wp-dyn/content/article/2006/06/16/AR2006061601766.html.

6. Rick Diamond and Mithra Moezzi, *Changing Trends: A Brief History of the US Household Consumption of Energy, Water, Food, Beverages and Tobacco*, Lawrence Berkeley National Laboratory publication date unknown, circa 2003, http.//epb.lbl.gov/homepages/Rick_Diamond/LBNL55011-trends.pdf.

7. Howard E. Vos, *New Illustrated Bible Manners and Customs*, (Nashville: Thomas Nelson, 1999), 13–14.

8. Ibid., 14.

9. Ibid., 133.

10. Ibid., 143–44.

11. Ibid., 142–43.

12. Ibid., 208.

13. Ibid.

14. Ibid., 247.

15. Ibid., 445–46.

16. Ibid., 464.

17. Ibid., 380–81.

18. Ibid., 534.

19. Ibid., 572.

20. Nancy Pearcey, "Is Love Enough? Recreating the Economic Base of the Family," published by the Rockford Institute Center on the Family in America; January 1990, vol. 4, no. 1., http://www.leaderu.com/orgs/arn/pearcey/np_family inamerica.htm.

21. Matthews, *"Just a Housewife,"* 6–7.

22. Ibid., 21.

23. Ibid., 43–44.

24. Ibid., 49.

25. Ibid., 50–51.

26. Nancy Pearcey, *Total Truth: Liberating Christianity from Its Cultural Captivity* (Wheaton: Crossway Books), 336.

27. Ibid., 333.

28. Ibid., 334.

29. Matthews, *"Just a Housewife,"* 117.

30. Danielle Crittenden, *What Our Mothers Didn't Tell Us* (New York: Touchstone, 1999), 128.

31. Matthews, "*Just a Housewife*," 142.

32. Ibid., 140–41.

33. Ibid., 170–71.

34. Ibid., 203.

35. Ibid., 210.

Chapter 6: The Mommy Wars

1. Mir Kamin, posted on March 15, 2008, http://www.blogher.com/more-mommy-wars-leslie-bennetts-and-secret-life-soccer-mom-raising-hackles.

2. Helaine Olen, "A Truce in the 'Mommy Wars,'" Salon.com, March 15, 2006, http://www.salon.com/mwt/feature/2006/03/15/mommy_wars/index.html.

3. Ann Crittenden, *The Price of Motherhood* (New York: Henry Holt, 2001), 11–12.

4. Hirshman, "Homeward Bound," *The American Prospect*.

5. Christopher Farrell, "The High Cost of the Mommy Tax," *BusinessWeek*, March 2, 2001,http://www.businessweek.com/bwdaily/dnflash/mar2001/nf2001032_060.htm.

6. Crittenden, *The Price of Motherhood*, 51.

7. Nancy F. Cott, *Public Vows: A History of Marriage and the Nation* (Cambridge: Harvard Univ., 2000), 11–12.

8. Crittenden, *The Price of Motherhood*, 55.

9. Ibid., 58, 60.

10. Charlotte Perkins Gilman, *Women and Economics* (Boston: Small, Maynard & Co., 1900), 14.

11. Ibid., 270–72.

12. Charlotte Perkins Gilman, "Females," *Suffrage Songs and Verses* (New York: Charlton, 1911), 10–11, http://digital.library.upenn.edu/women/gilman/suffrage/su-females.html.

13. Crittenden, *The Price of Motherhood*, 62.

14. Pearcey, *Total Truth*, 342.

15. Charlotte Perkins Gilman, *The Living of Charlotte Perkins Gilman: An Autobiography* (Salem, NH: Ayer Co, 1987, reprint edition), 163.

16. Crittenden, *Price of Motherhood*, 63.

17. Margaret Sanger, *Woman and the New Race* (New York: Brentano's, 1920), 63.

18. Deborah G. Felder, *The 100 Most Influential Women of All Time* (New York: Citadel Press, 1996), 12.

19. Ibid., 13.

20. Estelle Freedman, *The Essential Feminist Reader* (New York: Modern Library, 2007), 214.

21. Ibid., 213.

22. Margaret Sanger, *The Pivot of Civilization* (Whitefish, MT: Kessinger Publishing, 2004), 15.

23. Sanger, *Woman and the New Race*, 174.

24. Ibid., 185.

25. Ibid., 232–34.

26. Felder, *100 Most Influential Women*, 14.

27. Letter to Julia Ward Howe, October 16, 1873, recorded in Howe's diary at Harvard University Library, http://www.feministsforlife.org/history/foremoth.htm.

28. Marvin Olasky with Lynn Vincent, "Choosing Children Over Choice," *World*, January 26, 2008, http://www.worldmag.com/articles/13709.

29. Marvin Olasky, *Abortion Rites* (Wheaton: Crossway Books, 1991), 57.

30. Ibid., 62–63.

31. *Proceedings of the Free Convention, Rutland, Vermont, July 25–27, 1858* (Boston: J. B. Yerrinton, 1858), 9, as quoted in *Abortion Rites*, 67.

32. Jessica Wadkins, Trudy Chun, and Catherina Hurlburt, "The History of Abortion," published by Concerned Women for America, December 1, 1999, http://www.cwfa.org/articledisplay.asp?id=1416&department=CWA&categoryid=lif.

33. Eileen McDonagh, *Breaking the Abortion Deadlock: From Choice to Consent* (New York: Oxford University Press, 1996), 6–7.

34. Julia Duin, "India's Imbalance of Sexes," *Washington Times*, February 26, 2007.

35. Julia Duin, "GE Machines Used to Break the Law," *Washington Times*, February 28, 2007.

36. Catherine Bruton, "My Daddy's Name Is Donor," *Times* Online, December 13, 2007, http://women.timesonline.co.uk/tol/life_and_style/women/families/article3041127.ece.

37. "Bio-ethical Challenges for the 21st Century," transcript of a television interview with Fr. Frank Pavone's EWTN series, *Defending Life*, broadcast in 2000, http://www.priestsforlife.org/media/nathansoninterview.htm.

38. Sylvia Ann Hewlett, *Creating a Life: Professional Women and the Quest for Children* (New York: Talk Miramax Books, 2001), 9.

39. Lukas, *Politically Incorrect Guide to Women, Sex, and Feminism*, 114.

40. Ibid., 108–9.

41. Associated Press wire story, "Rising Number of Childless Women," October 24, 2003, http://www.cbsnews.com/stories/2003/10/24/national/main579973.shtml.

42. Köstenberger, *God, Marriage, and Family*, 112–13.

43. "Beyond Bottles and Diapers" sidebar, *Washington Post*, March 8, 2008.

Chapter 7: Raunch Culture Rip-Off

1. Associated Press wire story, "'Girls Gone Wild' Founder Joe Francis: Spitzer Call Girl in Video Archives; $1 Million Offer Pulled," Wednesday, March 19, 2008, http://www.foxnews.com/story/0,2933,339075,00.html.

2. Ariel Levy, "Ariel Levy on 'Raunch Culture,'" *The Independent UK*, December 4, 2005, http://www.independent.co.uk/news/uk/this-britain/ariel-levy-on-raunch-culture-517878.html.

3. Ariel Levy, "Dispatches from *Girls Gone Wild*," Slate.com, March 22, 2004, http://www.slate.com/id/2097485/entry/2097496/.

4. Levy, "Ariel Levy on 'Raunch Culture,'" *The Independent UK*.

5. Wendy Shalit, *Girls Gone Mild* (New York: Random House, 2007), xxiv–xxv.

6. Donna Freitas, "Sex Education," *Wall Street Journal*, April 4, 2008, W11, http://online.wsj.com/article/SB120728447818789307.html?mod=taste_primary_hs.

7. Ibid.

8. CDC press release issued at the 2008 National STD Prevention Conference, March 11, 2008, http://www.cdc.gov/STDConference/2008/media/release-11march2008.htm.

9. Jane C. Murphy, "The Third Wave," *Baltimore Sun* op-ed, March 24, 2008, http://www.baltimoresun.com/news/opinion/oped/bal-op.women24mar24,0,500379.story.

10. Betsy Israel, *Bachelor Girl* (New York: William Morrow, 2002), 120.

11. Ibid., 116.

12. Havelock Ellis, *Studies on the Psychology of Sex, Vol. 3*, originally published in 1913; 1926 revised edition archived on the Project Gutenberg eBook, http://www.gutenberg.org/files/13612/13612-h/13612-h.htm#3_THE_SEXUAL_IMPULSE_IN_WOMEN.

13. Havelock Ellis, *The Task of Social Hygiene* (Boston: Houghton Mifflin, 1912), 257.

14. Ibid., 248.

15. Margaret Sanger Biographical Sketch, courtesy of the Margaret Sanger Papers Project of New York University, as archived on http://www.nyu.edu/projects/sanger/secure/aboutms/index.html.

16. Pearcey, *Total Truth*, 142–43.

17. Ibid., 143.
18. Matthews, *"Just a Housewife,"* 213.
19. Donald A. Downs, contributor, "Pornography," Microsoft® Encarta® Online Encyclopedia 2007, http://encarta.msn.com.
20. Unattributed, "Women's War on Porn," *Time*, August 27, 1979, http://www.time.com/time/magazine/article/0,9171,920580-1,00.html.
21. "Fatal Addiction: Ted Bundy's Final Interview," Focus on the Family Films, 1989.
22. Barbara Ryan, *Feminism and the Women's Movement: Dynamics of Change in Social Movement Ideology and Activism* (New York: Routledge, 1992), 115.
23. Eliza Strickland, "Just Desserts," SFWeekly.com, March 29, 2006, http://www.sfweekly.com/2006-03-29/news/just-desserts/.
24. Ariel Levy, *Female Chauvinist Pigs: Women and the Rise of Raunch Culture* (New York: Free Press, 2005), 63.
25. David Amsden, "Not Tonight, Honey, I'm Logging On," *New York*, October 13, 2003.
26. Naomi Wolf, "The Porn Myth," *New York*, October 20, 2003.
27. Ibid.
28. C. J. Mahaney, *Sex, Romance and the Glory of God: What Every Christian Husband Needs to Know* (Wheaton, IL: Crossway Books, 2004), 73.
29. Ibid., 14.
30. Carolyn Mahaney, *Feminine Appeal* (Wheaton: Crossway, 2003), 83.
31. Shalit, *Girls Gone Mild*, 26–27.
32. Daniel Akin, *God on Sex* (Nashville: Broadman & Holman, 2003), 149.

Chapter 8: Feminine Faith

1. John Piper, Together for the Gospel 2008, Panel Discussion 6, recorded on April 17, 2008 in Louisville, KY.
2. Steven Tracy, "A Corrective to Distortions and Abuses of Male Headship," *Journal of Biblical Manhood and Womanhood*, vol. 8, no. 1, spring 2003, http://www.cbmw.org/Journal/Vol-8-No-1/A-Corrective-to-Distortions-and-Abuses-of-Male-Headship.
3. J. Ligon Duncan and Susan Hunt, *Women's Ministry in the Local Church* (Wheaton, IL: Crossway Books, 2006), 42.
4. Phillip R. Johnson, "A Wolf in Sheep's Clothing: How Charles Finney's Theology Ravaged the Evangelical Movement," 1998, archived on http://www.spurgeon.org/~phil/articles/finney.htm.
5. Margaret Köstenberger, *Jesus and the Feminists: Who Do They Say That He Is?* (Wheaton: Crossway, 2008), 15.

6. Beverly Zink-Sawyer, *From Preachers to Suffragists* (Louisville: Westminster John Knox Press, 2003), 30.
7. Mary A. Kassian, *The Feminist Mistake: The Radical Impact of Feminism on Church and Culture* (Wheaton: Crossway, 2005), 31–32.
8. Gary Dorrien, "American Liberal Theology: Crisis, Irony, Decline, Renewal, Ambiguity," *CrossCurrents*, June,] 2005.
9. Kassian, *The Feminist Mistake*, 180.
10. Ibid., 183.
11. Wayne Grudem, *Evangelical Feminism: A New Path to Liberalism?* (Wheaton: Crossway, 2006), 33.
12. John MacArthur, "The Biblical Position on Women's Roles," published in booklet form by Grace Community Church of Sun Valley, CA, and reprinted with permission on the Bible Bulletin Board of Columbus, NJ, http://www.biblebb.com/files/MAC/womensroles.htm.

OVER ONE-HALF MILLION SOLD

LIES
W●MEN
BELIEVE
AND THE TRUTH THAT SETS THEM FREE

FOREWORD BY ELISABETH ELLIOT

NANCY LEIGH DeMOSS

ISBN-13: 978-0-8024-7296-0

Satan is the master deceiver, and his lies are endless. Nancy tackles many of the falsehoods that deceive Christian women with alarming frequency and severity. She confronts these lies with practical truths found in Scripture, helping women to face the realities of this life with freedom and true joy.

 MOODY
PUBLISHERS.

1-800-678-8812 · MOODYPUBLISHERS.COM